The
Performance
Culture

The Performance Culture

Go Beyond Buzzwords to Lead Teams That Win

Khalil Smith
with Chris Weller

WILEY

Library of Congress Cataloging-in-Publication Data

Names: Smith, Khalil, author.
Title: The performance culture: go beyond buzzwords to lead teams that win / Khalil Smith ; with Chris Weller.
Description: First edition. | Hoboken, NJ : Wiley, [2025] | Includes bibliographical references and index.
Identifiers: LCCN 2024031455 (print) | LCCN 2024031456 (ebook) | ISBN 9781394270507 (hardback) | ISBN 9781394270521 (adobe pdf) | ISBN 9781394270514 (epub)
Subjects: LCSH: Leadership. | Organizational effectiveness.
Classification: LCC HD57.7 .S6483 2025 (print) | LCC HD57.7 (ebook) | DDC 658.4/092—dc23/eng/20240801
LC record available at https://lccn.loc.gov/2024031455
LC ebook record available at https://lccn.loc.gov/2024031456

Cover Design: Wiley
Cover Image: Courtesy of the Authors
Author Photo: Courtesy of Khalil Smith
SKY10092521_120224

To everyone who has taught, supported, advised, lifted, and cared for me. Your fingerprints are on my life, on my career, and on this book.

I know who you are, and you know who you are.

Thank you.

Contents

Introduction

Work isn't working.

As different as we are, in terms of what we value, what we enjoy, what we dream about, and wish for, one of the things we tend to share, probably even more so if you are reading this book, is that we work.

We may work mostly at home, in an office, in a local coffee shop, on the road with customers, in a warehouse, or somewhere else altogether. Whether we work for a small company or a large one, a month-old start-up or a family business passed down through generations, millions of us go to work with teams of people seeking to accomplish tasks that we couldn't achieve on our own.

But there's a problem.

In far too many instances, it feels like there are key parts of work that are broken. Too many people work on teams where they regularly feel unfulfilled, under-appreciated, lack clarity around the intended outcomes of the group, and, importantly, uncertain how they fit into the entire system. Many of us grapple with the question, *Is this really all there is?*

Each of us bears some degree of responsibility for figuring out how to solve the challenges our current world of work has brought, especially as work continues to change and evolve. Much of the work nowadays is less about using one's hands to make a product, and much more about using one's mind to improve that product. Even in many of the jobs where the labor is primarily manual, leaders have learned that the people closest to the work and challenges also tend to be the people closest to the solutions and insights. Leaders have a unique opportunity, perhaps even an obligation, to use their position of authority to help shape a workplace where those solutions and insights are focused on helping the company and unlocking potential.

And yet, for many of us, work just isn't working.

But let me be clear: I do not believe that work is broken beyond repair. If anything, I'm incredibly optimistic, and I'm inspired by how well we as employees have found our individual and collective voices, and are now sharing what matters to us. Through feedback and active participation, core elements like benefits, autonomy, and respect have continued to become the standard in so many workplaces.

So, this is not an apocalyptic manifesto, but rather a hopeful narrative, to support leaders of all levels of experiences and seniority with executing what's increasingly become a delicate balancing act: supporting the running of a successful business while also encouraging employees to bring the fullest and most productive parts of themselves to work.

For leaders, this is all done while navigating the fact that workforces have gotten more diverse along a tremendous number of dimensions; our companies have gotten larger and more global, and the issues we face require more specialized forms of knowledge. While it can be tempting to look back on the days of assembly lines and iron mills, and romanticize how easy work once seemed, leaders at those times believed their challenges were consuming and frustrating then as well. To be sure, many of the things leaders deal with today are different, and some might argue that today's leadership challenges are more ambiguous and less definitive. But being a leader has never felt easy. How does a leader decide how they might allow for a space for employees to talk about politics in the workplace, and whether to shut down conversations when others start them? How does a leader unite people despite the numerous sources of conflict and division that surround so many topics in today's workplace discussions? Gone are the days when many employees operated with an unspoken, though sometimes explicit, agreement not to talk about sensitive topics at work because "we keep things strictly business around here." But in blurring those lines and allowing these sensitive discussions into the workplace, what now?

If you're a leader today, you have a responsibility to create the optimal workplace for employees to thrive and be productive. That requires a degree of reflection about what you believe, why you believe it, and how you can translate the goals of the company into specific actions and realities for the people who work with you.

For many, the allure of leadership has all but faded. I speak with organizations that express how they are struggling to find great people who want to take the step into management, because the work of being a people leader is more complex, dynamic, and harder to "get right" than their role as an individual contributor. In some instances, people managers are expected to balance per- forming their own work and deliverables while also man- aging the work of others. In other instances, managers are completely removed from the daily tasks that made up so much of what they enjoyed and were good at when they were individual contributors. These leaders are meant to translate strategy and vision from their senior leaders and escalate concerns and resource requests from the teams they lead. Middle managers are, well, stuck in the middle. Add to this that we as employees expect our managers to be competent, knowledgeable about the business, vulnerable and human, but not overly fallible, and genuinely supportive of our needs and development, all of which can vary widely from person to person. No wonder so many individual contributors look at the responsibilities of management and say, "No thank you."

There are still lots of talented people stepping in to lead, and the competition for senior leadership doesn't seem to have suffered the same shaking of confidence as first-line managers. But leading is hard, and leading well is even harder. At the same time, leaders are getting a diverse set of messages from a diverse set of employees. Some employees just want to show up and do their job. They may want a paycheck, some fulfillment, and a little peace and quiet. They may get opportunities to express themselves through a variety of other outlets, and their desire is to work for a company that is healthy, financially stable, and fair. Others see work as a place where they are eager to share a broader and more immersive look into who they are. They may want to work for a company that openly and loudly supports their values, trumpets their points of view, and uses the scale and reach of the company to effect change in their community.

To whom should the leader listen? Who's on the right path?

Many leaders are ill-equipped to handle these tensions. Without the pull of higher compensation, greater status, or better job security, becoming a manager can feel like a waste of time, and perhaps that the job is set up to fail. There are certainly plenty of rewards to leadership, but given all of the challenges involved, many people are forced to ask themselves: Is it worth it?

Whether you keep reading this book or exit here depends on if you care about being a better leader. If you don't actually care about leading people, creating value, or unlocking potential and turning it into performance, then this book may be interesting, but it won't be applicable, and it certainly won't be transformational.

If, however, you are eager to continue your journey toward leading better teams, then we're in for an interesting ride together. Leadership isn't a box to check, like paying taxes. It's not something you can schedule for a particular day and time, and otherwise ignore. That kind of thought is what shows up in focusing on annual appraisals, but forgetting about the everyday interactions, conversations, and investments that go into being respected and showing others that same respect. If you're a leader today, your job is an ongoing practice, a garden that needs constant watering, sunlight, fertilizer, weeding, and general care and attention. Your job isn't to keep addressing problems within your team, or even to learn better techniques for addressing problems. You want to avoid the problems altogether so that you can focus on your real job: leading. In practice, that means creating the conditions for your employees to succeed in their respective roles, with the hope that the company as a whole benefits from these aligned efforts.

Now is also a useful time to be specific about the type of leadership I'm talking about. Yes, there are leaders in every part of the business. There are people without formal leadership titles who can be more impactful in your company than the most senior leaders. There are people without budgets who actually control where money is directed and who gets what resources. There are undercurrents of influence that flow beneath the surface of the more formal leadership hierarchy that shows up on organizational charts and succession planning presentations.

While these concepts are useful to the project manager who wants to run more inclusive meetings, and the graphic designer who wants to streamline the process to go from idea to execution, the people with the greatest responsibility for the culture and performance of the company are those to whom that responsibility has been given. People leaders, managers, and executives have stepped forward and said that they will lead. They have opted into the trials and challenges of building and maintaining a company that is resilient and high performing. And as such, many times they receive a disproportionately large share of the rewards and the responsibility. I'm talking to them. While we all *can* lead, leaders *must* lead. They must reinforce and reward the right behaviors. They must manage and minimize the wrong behaviors. And above all they must model, in words and especially in actions, what they expect from others. Modeling behaviors requires a level of self-development and intention that can be both enriching and challenging. Leadership is not a profession, but it is a role that so many before you have embraced.

There are commonalities across what great leadership looks and feels like, regardless of the conditions. Leaders bring people together from a variety of backgrounds. Leaders ensure that people have what they need to be successful. Leaders create teams out of individuals. Leadership across the ages is anchored, in part, on diverse team members, relevant resources, and the opportunity to contribute. Yet there may be no three words more misunderstood in the working world than these three: *diversity*, *equity, and inclusion.* Those three words, abbreviated as DEI, have become a hotbed of discussion, misuse, misunderstanding, and misapplication. Along with DEI, words like *justice, fairness, belonging, equality, allyship,* and a host of other terms have risen in prominence. Along with that increase has come concern about exactly what they mean, not just in concept, but in practice. Words initially used to help teams work better together have in some instances become buzzwords – terms that can confuse people more than they clarify important aspects of work. When understood properly, as a performance amplifier, DEI is the heart of culture, and culture is the heart of high-performing teams and companies.

This book is a reference to support all leaders to help people work together and accomplish more, together.

Culture is often misunderstood as something done "over there," in the domain of human resources. In reality, the behaviors and concepts that are the foundation of effective cultures are as integral to the success of a business as are other important functions, like marketing or finance. Just as a well-run company has its chief marketing officer or someone in a similar role to focus on the company's brand, and the chief financial officer to pay special attention to its revenue, margins, and bottom line, many companies have experts or teams focused on culture. And just like marketing and finance, culture cannot live in a silo if it has any chance of being effective. A company where only marketing is concerned with the brand cannot build a world-class brand. A company where only finance is attentive to what's earned and spent cannot be a fiscally responsible company. It's the same with culture. Infusing culture back into the overall strategy of the company is paramount to unlocking the benefits and capitalizing on the potential energy of the workforce. Clarity around what is affecting your team, what people care about, and what challenges are influencing people's ability to deliver on the purpose of the company are all things that need to matter to every leader. And being able to remove obstacles is the responsibility of every leader.

The research is clear: Diverse and inclusive teams, all the way from small groups to large companies, tend to outperform teams that are either more homogenous, less inclusive, or both.[1] The challenge for leaders is figuring out how to grab as many of those benefits for themselves as they can, on a consistent basis. This book offers you a solution to that problem – your ticket to creating high-performing cultures where people find meaning and satisfaction in their work, and the organization as a whole thrives. That solution is the ABCS of culture. A for awareness, the act of identifying a gap, learning about the opportunity, and educating oneself and others on the facts of the matter. B for behaviors, the concrete and tangible actions that are purposely fit to address the opportunity. C for community, building a coalition that expands the number and strength of the supporters. S for systems, the processes, policies, and procedures that root the change deep in the foundation of rewards and performance management that help drive behavior.

This book is the culmination of more than two decades of my personal learning, along with a host of truisms, experiences, and wisdom shared from a wide variety of leaders and individual contributors across industries, company sizes, tenure, and just about every demographic difference. These lessons have happened while working with and consulting with a host of companies, from Fortune 500 behemoths whose influence moves whole industries, to start-ups ready to change the world with a small team and a big idea. I've learned as much from observing incredible leaders and impeccably run teams, departments, and divisions as I have learned from really challenged leaders and teams that were on the verge of imploding. My goal is to bring that learning together into principles and practices that can support you on your leadership journey, no matter whether you're at the start, the middle, or getting ready to pass the reins to the next leaders. Each chapter in this book will teach you the theory, science, and the practice of the ABCS, so that you can understand them, communicate them to others in ways that are easily digestible, and start using them right away. And once you're finished with your first read-through, you can open this book back up and jump to any section where you might want another jolt of information or inspiration.

There are some things this book won't do. It won't help executives clarify the vision or values of their company. It won't tell frontline managers how to improve hiring or write and deliver better performance reviews. And it won't guide you toward creating the most progressive or boundary-pushing organization. Those are different books, and there are some great ones out there. Consider this book your copilot for creating the best cultures possible – teams that perform at a level you never could have imagined because everyone is aligned in what matters most, carries out the behaviors that support those priorities, feels united and valued in the team's mission, and systematizes that which can run on autopilot.

This is the real promise of high-performing teams. This is what it means to collaborate well. This is how to create cultures that win.

CHAPTER 1

A Big Misunderstanding

Amid the debates over profits, politics, and buzzwords, we've missed work's best purpose.

You know those moments when an idea you've been wrestling with for a while suddenly comes into focus, and you see the world differently? After your perspective is shifted, and armed with the new information, you may wonder how you didn't see it before. That's what I hope we can collectively achieve in terms of how we view the nature of work.

A misunderstanding many of us hold about work is that work can only fulfill one of two roles. Either work ought to represent who we are completely – every nuance and idiosyncrasy, every preference and belief – or work represents none of who we are, merely a way to earn a living. Living on either end of that spectrum can be tempting, because it reduces the complexity to an all-or-nothing decision.

That kind of simplicity can be attractive, easier to grasp, and easier to rally around, because it doesn't require any subtlety. But I have found that either mindset can be the root of so many of the interpersonal disagreements that arise at work, and that when we operate with the *right* understanding, and calibrate our expectations and behaviors accordingly, many of those ideological problems begin to fade away, and many may cease to exist.

For example, it's so much easier to presume that identity is either everything at work, or that it is nothing. By making identity everything, we find ourselves running every word of every sentence through a lens of inclusion, and judging every interaction as a pass or fail. We start to see a meeting as either inclusive or not inclusive, with zero gradient, and lack the recognition that the same meeting may have been more inclusive along certain dimensions, while simultaneously being less inclusive along other dimensions. Similarly, we start to believe that our group or individual identity matters most. When we apply a lens of *identity as everything*, we contend that our gender, our sexual orientation, our physical abilities, our socioeconomic status, or a host of other characteristics are the totality of what make us who we are. And since each of us is a unique blend of so many points of intersection, we can start to believe that no one else can ever understand our distinctive experience, which means nobody can really appreciate who we are as people. Through that lens, it becomes clear how so many well-intentioned employees fall down a path of finger-pointing, frustration, and isolation.

The other side of this spectrum is that identity is nothing. To presume that identity holds no value is to say that there is no value in the experience of being marginalized or overlooked, or any benefit in being in a place that feels safe and supportive. By vilifying identity and turning it into a caricature of its true intentions, anyone who shares a piece of their identity or explains their needs risks appearing like someone just looking for sympathy, an edge, or a handout. If identity is nothing, then all that matters is working hard, because the system is fair and it will reward skill and hard work, regardless of any other factors.

As with most overly simplistic models, the all-or-nothing dichotomy of work is incorrect, polarizing, and misguided. Identity is neither everything nor nothing; it is *something*. It plays a significant role at work, but that significance need not swallow up other priorities of the business or get thrown out as frivolous. Even if our work lives and personal lives are distinct, what happens at work is influenced by what happens outside.

Consider, for instance, how what happens in broader society has traditionally affected what happens inside work. Failures to recognize institutionalized biases and asymmetries in housing, transportation, healthcare, and so many other facets of life, mirror how they've played out in hiring, investment, development, promotion, and an array of other opportunities in businesses across the world. Bias is wherever people are. We may have biases about height, age, religion, caste, skin tone, whether someone smokes, and a host of other differences, in addition to the more frequently discussed biases around differences like gender and ethnicity. We do well to recognize that society and business affect each other, and that bias outside of work can negatively influence what happens at work.

Yet we must be cautious not to confuse our desired outcomes of greater fairness with thinking that businesses are responsible for those outcomes everywhere. Businesses need to make work fair and equitable, and their obligation ends there.

In my own career, I can vividly recall two pivotal moments that shaped my understanding of how our personal lives can intersect with our work lives in subtle but meaningful ways.

When I was still early in my career as a people leader in a retail environment, having been freshly given responsibility for leading, managing, inspiring, and developing a team of incredible people, I kept myself relatively closed off to those around me. I didn't really ask about their motivations for the job, and I was equally quiet about sharing my own. I'm sure there were a host of reasons, but the ones that I most strongly associate are that I was younger than most of my fellow store managers, one of the only racial minorities in my peer group, and, as far as I could tell, one of the only managers who had not completed four years of higher education. Each of those differences was important to me, and since I feared so strongly the idea of being judged, I tended to put all of my effort into always being the best in the room. I wanted to be the most well-read, and so I consumed books on business and leadership. I put my energy into being the best dressed, and so I wore slacks, dress shoes, and blazers, while my peers were quite comfortable in sneakers and flats and t-shirts. And beyond not sharing details of my personal life, I was intentional about not sharing anything that might hint at what I valued, or who I was, because in my mind that might mean someone would have something to use against me, or that they might see me differently.

For the most part, this didn't tend to matter much. I had my amazing wife and first son at home, a close set of friends, and I was, dare I say, pretty good at my job. My team made our business goals, delighted our customers, and by most metrics we were successful. But what hit me was when we did a regular employee sentiment survey, and the results came back showing that some people

thought I was fake. Others thought I was so overly pol-
ished that it had to be an act. Others questioned why I was
always so positive and happy. I was crushed. I brought the
results to my mentor, and he looked me square in the eye
and said that for as much as my teams and I were getting
right, I approached leadership like I was reading it from
the back of a business book.

Now, I'd love to say that moment was the catalyst
I needed to find my true center, define my personal values, and emerge as the leader I wanted to be, but in my
experience that kind of immediate growth usually only
happens in the movies. I had my revelation, but I didn't
yet have my path forward. So, over the next few months
I did my best to open up, listen more, and appropriately
share who I was and what I valued. Slowly, I stopped
hearing comments like, "I feel like I don't really know who
you are." This, for me, was what I needed to propel me to
better understand how I could be myself, not feel the need
to hold back pieces that informed my perspective and my
leadership style, and help others to trust not just my directions, but trust me as a person.

From that experience, I learned how much trust truly
matters, because when employees have choices about their
job, they want to know that those leading them are human,
and care about the team they're charged with leading.

In the second example, I learned how much my own
humanity affects how I do my job, often in subtle and
pernicious ways.

As the store manager of a massive flagship store, with
more than 500 employees and more than $100 million
in annual revenue, I had a decent amount of latitude.
While my goal was always to support our policies, support our employees, and deliver a great experience to

every customer, there were times when a decision, like whether to return a damaged item or not, was a matter of judgment. *My* judgment. Many such decisions depended on a number of factors, like the condition of the product, time since the purchase, the precedent a manager believed the decision would set, the demeanor of the customer, and even the emotional state of the manager.

What I realized was that when I saw someone of a particular size, build, gender, skin tone, and demeanor come into the store, I found myself gravitating toward them, and eager to do what we could to deliver an even slightly better experience. But it wasn't people who were wealthy or attractive or tall that triggered the gravitational pull – although those are all traits that can trigger our biases. It was men who reminded me of my father! As soon as a bald, dark-skinned guy with a huge smile on his face and a little bit of a belly (sorry Dad!) came into the store, I was ready with a smile and an eagerness to deliver an amazing experience. I never did anything outside of policy, or anything that would be considered inappropriate, but there sometimes was that slight bit more. That gentle bend toward saying yes. That extra motivation to make this person happy.

That realization set me on a path of seeking to understand psychology and bias, and how I could bring all of those together to both manage my own biases, and to create visibility and practices for mitigating bias at the organizational level. While a 5% price discount on a floor model in a retail store probably won't materially change someone's life, a slightly higher raise might. A slightly greater chance at promotion might matter. More latitude to try and fail, knowing there's a greater degree of support, might matter. My bias certainly wasn't intentional, but

I had to recognize that my intention didn't matter, because my impact was suboptimal.

These two stories meant a dramatic change in how I saw the world, and how much I appreciated the ways that the personal can quickly bleed into the professional. Can you recall an aspect of your personal life or identity that directly influences how you do your job? Something you can't just ignore, because losing that would negatively impact some aspect of what makes you great at what you do? If you are a leader, can you think of those traits in the people you lead?

Remember, your job isn't to bring out *every* virtuous trait in your employees. Avoid the trap of thinking that the culture you create must either represent all of whom your employees are as individuals, and that it should be optimized and customized around each person, or that it must represent none of who they are, and that work functions only as a way to make money.

The truth is that an optimal role of business is to care for the health and sustainability of the business itself, to care for the people who work for the business, and to invest in people to such an extent that each of us can return to our personal lives with positivity and energy, and can use our talents and passions in ways that are important to us. Put simply, businesses are not governments, and we should not take whatever failures or opportunities we may perceive in government, and delegate those responsibilities to businesses. Government is responsible for ensuring that all its citizens are treated equally, with fairness and representation. It's also accountable – in theory, at least – for providing a basic standard of living, and allocating resources so that the most fortunate of us are not so removed from the least fortunate of us. When we take these obligations and transfer them to private businesses, we conflate the goals of business with the function of government.

When we recognize this misunderstanding, we start to see the reach of its collateral damage throughout working life. If business is responsible for society, then it makes sense that we get into disagreements in our place of business about societal issues, such as identity, word choice, intentions, political issues, and more. All of these discussions are incredibly worthwhile and need to be resolved, but generally not at work. Much of making the world as fair as possible is the responsibility of civic life, outside the purview of the team's goals. While many high-ranking and high-profile leaders may call on people to "bring your full self to work," the more appropriate directive might be to bring one's full *work self* to work.

For large chunks of human history, life on Earth has gotten objectively better.[1] Today, we tend to live longer, enjoy more resources, and have greater opportunities for a full and healthy life than people in past decades and centuries. There are clearly significant exceptions to this trend – for instance, subjective measures like happiness and fulfillment have recently begun to decline.[2] But ever since the scientific revolution, and later the age of enlightenment, humans have advanced by leaps and bounds in medicine, public health, engineering, and technology. We used to wonder about what was happening at the molecular level or the scale of interplanetary movement, and then brilliant minds invented microscopes and telescopes to uncover what felt like secrets of the universe, but were in fact just beyond our perception. These things were always there, but invisible to the naked eye. A similar kind of progress has happened at work. We have more insight than ever, in the form of social science research, case studies, and mounds of data into the ways humans function and how we work best together. And, just like how atoms and planets have always behaved the same way whether we knew it or not, there have always been truisms about how people work best, create the best teams, perform work under optimal conditions, and deliver stellar results.

Just because we didn't have brain scans and cortisol measures for workers in a paper mill hundreds of years ago doesn't mean the workers weren't stressed out. As they say, perception lags reality.

This applies equally to our understanding of how social phenomena, such as innovation, happen. Factory workers used to be viewed primarily as resources on an assembly line. Now, with qualitative and quantitative data gathering, we know that people close to the end product very often have the clearest view of inefficiencies in the process.[3] They are up close, so they know where small optimization can lead to massive gains in productivity and revenue. Good leaders ask these workers questions, listen to their answers, and seriously consider implementing their suggestions. Workers aren't more correct today than they were before, but now we know that the title of "leader" is not always synonymous with being correct. We recognize that asking questions is not a sign of weakness. We've gotten wiser, and when we're at our best, we use that wisdom to allow our teams and companies to achieve outcomes on a scale that would have seemed incomprehensible not too long ago.

But now we've started overreaching. We've taken a solid hypothesis – *Work done by humans must consider the needs of those humans* – and begun to apply it in places where it's unnecessary, or actually counterproductive.

It's as if we're now saying that all work must consider the individual needs, preferences, desires, and beliefs of the people doing the work, above and beyond the goals of the task at hand.

Yet again, the alternate view – that work is work, and the human is a replaceable cog in a grand machine – is equally alarming in how damaging it can be to the individual and to the organization. Either set of actions, infantilizing and coddling or neglecting and exploiting, are paths to underperformance at the level of the individual and the level of the organization.

Some of the modern DEI movement has sought to put an emphasis on matters of identity, such as age, gender, sexual orientation, ethnicity, ability, and neurodiversity. Within each group, there are important topics that reflect the very real challenges these groups have experienced with regard to securing equal rights in society. These can, and should, play out in the benefits an employer provides – for example, same-sex couples enjoying the parental leave benefits enjoyed by heterosexual couples, adoptive parents getting the same benefits as birthing parents, or providing appropriate healthcare benefits for transgender employees in the same way the company would for everyone else. These *are* the domain of business. Supporting core aspects of employees' personal care helps employees perform better in their respective roles, and that creates a win for the employee and a win for the employer.

Leaders must be attuned to the issues employees face, and they must create policies and practices that are inclusive to employees. Put simply, in an ideal work partnership, the company and each employee are clear about what they will realistically deliver to the other, *and that agreement is not all-encompassing.* It's simply not practical, nor the point of work, for every individual in a business to expect their preferred level of customization or optimization for every issue they may face. The role of business is to perform its purpose, provide value to shareholders, and uplift employees, but that stops short of applying resources toward creating the perfect version of society within its walls, where every issue influences how work gets done.

This is a well-intentioned, yet unsustainable, leap from the progress we've been making in including the voices and ideas from those who have been historically ignored, typically minorities and those on the margins. We often have an easier time seeing the boundaries from the other perspective – that is, the employer's. Most of us readily agree that employees don't owe their entire selves to the company. This book and the concepts within are based on the belief that this agreement goes both ways. In a mature workplace, employees are invested and engaged in seeing the company be successful, and the organization is invested in the same for its employees. This is a healthy, sustainable, and resilient model for business.

The beauty of refining our focus on people's personal beliefs and identities is that it requires no new solutions. Thousands of years ago, ancient armies and nation states were also hyper-focused on achieving their missions. These groups knew that teamwork wasn't just a collection of individuals, each person doing their own thing and a leader furiously trying to tie it all together at the end. They knew, as we know now, that teamwork is usually the combination of specialized team members working in concert, each fulfilling a specific and meaningful role. The ability to achieve this level of teamwork is just as important in today's corporations as it was in ancient Africa, Asia, Rome, or Greece.

What's changed is primarily what we call this essential business function, and the degree to which the importance and the language are the stuff of heated debates and fruitless bickering. As of this writing, the term of art is *DEI*, for diversity, equity, and inclusion. Before that, it was D&I. Before that, it went by civil rights and women's empowerment. Before that, it went by other labels, and after this period of time it will almost certainly be called something else.

What we call these efforts is arguably less important than the role they play. While there is value in being clear about what we mean when we talk with others, the value to organizations of what we currently call DEI won't change. DEI has always, and will always, represent the facets of the business through which we learn how high performance happens, and helping those charged with folding those insights back into the everyday running of the business. That's what this book prioritizes. We will spend time working through how to identify the issues that matter most for the healthy operation of your team, how to create behaviors that embody those priorities, how to build community around those shared behaviors, and how to embed systems that make those actions frictionless and permanent.

Our first big, shared truth is that work is work, not a replacement for direct government interaction, and not a mechanism for sweeping societal change. Our second shared truth is that identity is far too often misunderstood as either something that should be dismissed or something that should be revered, while the truth lies between those poles. These two shared truths lead us down a path of defining how we build cultures in our organizations in ways that are coherent and ultimately beneficial for employees and business outcomes. They help us leverage our differences as a performance amplifier.

When you're ready, it's time to start looking at the framework that will help you achieve this level of performance and create the kind of culture all of us deserve.

CHAPTER 2

The ABCS of Culture

*Appreciating the importance of awareness,
behaviors, community, and systems.*

Our ultimate aim is a company culture where each
employee is able to show up, do their work, bring
the relevant parts of themselves to the degree they feel
comfortable, and feel appreciated for helping the company achieve its goals. While there is no single solution
that will get us to that ideal company culture, or create
the optimal organization, there are steps we can take that
move us in that direction.

But first, let's linger on "optimal" for a moment.

The optimal organization doesn't look like an earthly
version of perfection, where everyone gets everything
they want all the time. It's not a workplace where everyone always agrees with everyone else, feels no stress over
deadlines, and achieves every company goal. The optimal organization I'm describing is rooted in reality. When
we view work through a more appropriate and accurate
lens – that to achieve our best requires understanding
aspects of what makes people unique and special, but

that it doesn't need to reflect every aspect of who we are – we free ourselves to drop so much of what's been weighing down our people and our conversations.

In order to know what does matter, though, we have to ask: What are the essential aspects of performance and culture building? What actions actually move the organization forward, with its employees as the driving force? From everything I've witnessed, read, studied, discussed, and learned over my career, building a great culture rests on four interdependent parts of a cycle, attended to on an ongoing basis: awareness, behaviors, community, and systems. Just about every other important element we may discuss at work and in meetings – accountability, resilience, impact, collaboration – is contained within one of these four priorities.

These are the ABCS of culture: Awareness. Behaviors. Community. Systems.

This model organizes and simplifies the actions that I've seen work across businesses of varying sizes, markets, complexities, and compositions. It's the idea that first, we need to decide that something is worth our time, and educate ourselves about where we are, where we'd like to be, and the gap between those things (Awareness), before taking the appropriate actions to bridge that gap (Behaviors). After that, the focus is on building a coalition of others who can both support the efforts and recognize the blind spots in our best intentions and plans (Community). Finally, we round out all of that work by building a collection of processes that ensure we'll be able to measure our progress and sustain our efforts, even as our initial passion or motivation may start to wane (Systems). And then we cycle back to the start and evaluate our efforts all over again, this time from a better starting point.

The ABCS model is not a quick fix. Knitting this model through a team or company won't be a straight line, like following the directions for assembling a piece of furniture. And similar to any change, there will be moments of immense success and moments of intense frustration. But more than other practices you might have tried in the past, employing these practices will take you where you want to go, if where you want to go includes shared commitment around high performance.

Awareness is the first step toward creating the optimal workplace experience. Awareness means getting educated about a topic before you attempt to do anything else. It's the part at the start of the journey where you're reading, observing, asking questions, and ensuring you understand enough about a topic to be able to explain it to someone else. If it's awareness about the experience of underrepresented talent on your team or in your company, this might take the shape of conversations, reading blogs, or listening to experts through podcasts and videos. This is your initial work to ensure that when you begin your next steps, you're doing so from a place of understanding. It's unrealistic to assume you will become a subject matter expert overnight, but you'll at least be able to ask better questions and provide more educated responses.

This period of awareness is exemplified by embracing a beginner's mindset and questioning what you may think you already know. This is in part because there is so much going on around us at all times, constantly. In order to cut through some of that stimuli, whether those are emails, customer calls, or meetings, you must pause, attend to a specific point of interest, and learn about it with a high degree of intention. For instance, when a community of employees are dealing with a specific concern, leaders need to educate themselves so that they can make informed decisions about what comes next. Acting without information often leads to misinterpretation, miscommunication, and in many cases disillusionment. Charging headfirst into the matter, trying to build or solve without first taking the time to comprehend the general shape of the issue, will likely lead to wasted effort.

Scientists across a range of disciplines, many who study how humans think, have given us tremendous insights over the past decades. One of the biggest insights is that our brains essentially take shortcuts in order to make sense of the world and ensure that we can find patterns among the deluge of sensory information the world throws at us. These shortcuts are known as cognitive biases.[1] One such cognitive bias is known as *naive realism*, or the false belief that others usually see the world in the same way that we do. Naive realism takes a variety of shapes in our everyday work worlds, such as attending a conference call and being confident that everyone left that call with the same beliefs, actions, and priorities that you did. That sense of, *Of course it's this way. How could any reasonable person believe otherwise?* is this bias at work. This can manifest as a belief that anyone who disagrees with your view of an issue is being intentionally obtuse, or simply lying. It can be extremely challenging to grasp that someone else viewed the same inputs through a different set of filters, accumulated over their lifetime of culture, education, and experiences, and came to a different conclusion.

The Awareness step in the ABCS is about piercing through that bias, and actively challenging your baseline assumptions about an unfamiliar issue. Being aware of our habits and preferences, aware of the experiences and needs of those around us, and aware of what we know and what we don't know, are all important in the journey toward building and maintaining a healthy, thriving workplace.

Behaviors are what you can see or hear. They're not intentions. They're not hopes. They are what you could record using your phone's video camera. Behaviors are actions and words. And they matter so much because they allow us to turn our intentions and hopes into real things that have an impact on the world around us. To go from "I want to be more inclusive" to "In every hour-long meeting, I will leave at least 10 minutes for contrary points of view, and will recognize and vocally appreciate the person who has raised a valid concern," is to go from a generic intention to a specific behavior that can be tracked and adjusted. Did I leave 10 minutes in that meeting? Did I thank a person who raised a contrary point of view? Did that get us the desired outcome of greater inclusion for most of the meeting attendees? What behavior should I tweak or evolve in order to achieve even more inclusion?

Community is bringing together the people around us to accomplish things we likely couldn't achieve on our own. Humans are socially wired to build networks. We've evolved to live and work in groups, and we deliver better long-term results when we collaborate with our group members on complex tasks.[2] Forming a community of people who will do similar work to continue raising their awareness, and are equally on board with identifying and taking action on key behaviors, means that we are building a group of people who can hold us accountable to the things we've said we're going to do. Deciding on your own to leave 10 minutes in every meeting for productive dissent is different than sharing the plan with your team, helping them to understand why you think this will increase inclusion, seeking their feedback on whether this is the right behavior, and encouraging them to keep you honest. Similarly, when the community then starts to adopt this behavior in their own meetings, we're getting closer to the tipping point of moving from an individual behavior to a community's practices. Indeed, it's at the Community stage where individual behaviors begin to transform into the thing we call a culture.

Systems are how we ensure culture doesn't remain a set of cognitively taxing decisions that we make each time, and instead becomes a default process where the most desired behaviors are at the center of every practice, policy, and procedure. Systems can be technology, such as customer relationship management software, or a practice, such as a policy to end meetings five minutes early to give people a break between back-to-back meetings. But systems all share the common goal of making the desired behavior harder *not* to do than any other, less desirable behavior.

For instance, let's say your company is adopting a system that overhauls your hiring processes and mandates that all interviewers ask a standard set of questions, and then complete an evaluation rubric with clearly defined criteria for success. Such a system means that all of a sudden it's easier to follow that system than it is to just interview someone and "go with your gut." The system has been designed and deployed to help find great talent, and as such, the path of least resistance is also the optimal path. Systems, whether technology, policies, rewards, or penalties, help shape behavior by carving a path through the company, and realizing that whatever we create as the default tends to have a tremendous impact on how any of us act in a given situation.

Deployed correctly, you can use the ABCS to build diverse and inclusive teams that outperform other teams. And the best part? Not only can you use it when you're faced with original, complex, and non-routine tasks and projects – it actually works *better* when the stakes are higher. When the stakes are higher, we are tempted to move quickly and confidently, but perhaps not always correctly or sustainably. A wonderful mentor used to remind me that "in times of stress, people revert to what made them successful." What he meant is that many times when we feel like we're facing a troubling situation, we naturally return to what we've seen or done previously, without pausing to consider whether the tried-and-true best practices are actually applicable to the scenario that's in front of us. The ABCS model counteracts that impulse. It introduces original thinking when it's needed most.

But why do we need all four parts of the ABCS model? To show you, let's start small, building up the model one element at a time. Here's what a team looks like if it has just one of the elements and none of the other three.

1. Awareness only: *I'm aware, but there's nothing I can, or will, do about it.*
2. Behaviors only: *I'm just going to try a bunch of stuff and see what works . . . if anything. If nothing works, or if things get a lot worse, then I'll try a bunch of other stuff.*
3. Community only: *Hey everyone, we're all in it together. I'm not quite sure what "it" is, but at least we're together!*

4. Systems only: *This vendor told me we need this, and our competitors are using it. So I bought it. And now we're going to use it.*

Now here's what it looks like if a team has just two:

1. Awareness and Behaviors: *I've got a good idea of what's going on, and what I need to do to change my own behavior, but everyone needs to do this work on their own, and perhaps eventually we'll meet up later.*

2. Awareness and Community: *We can see what's missing, and we're aligned around addressing it, but we know the problem and not the solution, and we're not in this for the long haul. Let's hold hands and hope this solves itself.*

3. Awareness and Systems: *I figured it out, and I'm single-handedly changing how we reward and penalize. You'll thank me later.*

4. Behaviors and Community: *Does everyone agree we should start doing something, without really understanding the implications or the possible ramifications? Great! Let's go.*

5. Behaviors and Systems: *It's already obvious what needs to get done, so I'll just go ahead and tie this deep into our processes and procedures. What could go wrong?*

6. Community and Systems: *Since none of us are willing to admit that we don't know what we're solving for, but we're all too nice or scared to say it, we'll make some long-term bets and commitments that bind us to a way of working. Go team!*

Finally, we can see how even missing just one element makes teams less stable and more vulnerable to performance challenges:

1. Awareness, Behaviors, and Community, but missing Systems: *We've done all the right things, but it's kind of like a New Year's resolution. We just can't seem to keep our focus when things get busy or challenging, and we're stuck in a cycle of getting things going, and then watching them fall apart when other priorities come up.*

2. Awareness, Behaviors, and Systems, but missing Community: *The senior leaders decided what we're going to do, and we have compliance, but not commitment. People do what we ask when we're watching, but there's no sense that if we were to stop monitoring, or suggest a change in course, that anyone would fight to keep what we've built.*

3. Awareness, Community, and Systems, but missing Behaviors: *We're getting there, but we're so inconsistent on what it's all supposed to look or sound like. We use lots of general language and overarching themes, but it's really up to each individual or smaller pockets within the larger team, to figure out what "good" is supposed to be.*

4. Behaviors, Community, and Systems, but missing Awareness: *We didn't take the time to educate ourselves on the issue at hand, so we're making mistakes that others have made and fumbling our way through something that we could have researched at the start. It's a sort of institutionalized ignorance.*

Each of these situations is happening right now in organizations. That's why it's important that you also see how getting all four elements right can radically transform an organization and bypass so much of the buzzword overload that plagues business practices today. With the ABCS, your team won't just feel more connected; you'll start seeing and feeling the changes. For example, when you find the right balance of the ABCS, you'll begin to hear more "we" language. That sounds like people coming together to solve issues and to coordinate around challenges that require a greater level of coordination. In addition, you should start to see less written communication focused on capturing information for the sake of having a record with which to push back on someone (e.g. "Per my prior email . . ."). Instead, you should see more written communication related to keeping the right people informed, and making sure the team is reducing reliance on any single point of failure.

You may also find, as the leader of the team, you're being pulled into fewer things, and people need your support in different ways than they have in the past. Why would this be the case? Imagine you're running a team of highly individualistic members who are focused on protecting their turf, looking good, and shining above everyone else. In this scenario, people are probably coming to you regularly. They come to you to tell you what they've done well. They come to you to tell you what others have messed up. They come to you to get answers to challenging issues, because they wouldn't dare ask someone else on the team who might use it against them. Basically, they come to you for everything.

Now envision this team, but instead they're a team of people who are learning to value and use the unique skills, background, and experience of their teammates, and they're working toward shared goals. In this new, more ideal, reality, your value as a leader changes from attending to the more tactical or routine tasks to weighing in on the more strategic concerns, and your greatest contribution is removing obstacles that the team perhaps cannot handle by themselves.

The beauty of this work is that while we are absolutely talking about DEI, leadership, and culture, we're also talking about performance. This work brings them all together. At the beginning and end of all of this, we're talking about what it takes to be a leader who sets their team up to succeed. How you invite and create space for difficult conversations. How you manage and embrace tension on your team. How you invite perspectives that are vastly different from your own, and combine those differences, not to erase or indoctrinate them, but to bring them together toward shared goals.

This work is seldom glamorous. It's effortful, and it often feels like friction – because it is. Your team shouldn't be smooth, like pureed baby food. It should be hearty, like a stew. And while that means things won't be uniform and neat, distinctiveness is what you want. You want individual elements to work together, so that the whole is greater than the sum of its parts. That doesn't happen by accident. And in many cases, it doesn't happen at all, since most people are never given a good set of guidelines for success. The ABCS are your set of guidelines for creating the culture you've always wanted.

A difficult truth every leader would do well to accept when they step into a position of influence is that this work of building a strong and productive culture is never done. You read that right. *This. Work. Is. Never. Done.*

When you feel like your team is composed of just the right type of representation, and operating at the perfect flow and pace, something will change. It's inevitable. A person will start to struggle. Someone will leave. Someone will join. The market will move. You'll recognize that there is another facet of diversity that has been missing from your team, which you'll realize is crucial to your ability to meet the needs of your stakeholders. And so, you'll start the cycle of Awareness, Behaviors, Community, and Systems over again. You may look through a slightly different lens, or ask someone with a different perspective about how you can continue to optimize your world of work. Then you'll redefine which behaviors are the right ones, based on what you've learned and explored in the Awareness phase. Then you'll build that new form of community, that new process of bringing people together and making sure that while folks are meant to be diverse in their demographics and perspectives, your team is still aligned in the *what* and the *why*. And then you'll bake all of this into your systems, to ensure that how you reward, recognize, correct, and punish are all pointed in the same direction as your words and your intentions.

In the beginning, I recommend you follow the ABCS in order. Notice how each element in the process depends on the element next to it. As you complete one full cycle, you may find you need to tweak behaviors before building new awareness, or that your community needs tending before you start a second cycle. Addressing the individual elements is something to embrace, not avoid. It's a sign you are gaining fluency with the ABCS and how they live within your team and organization.

To spark your thinking right away, let's look at two hypothetical scenarios. Even though the ABCS are new to you, I have a feeling you may recognize elements of these in your own workplace, and begin to form ideas for how the ABCS might help you solve your problems.

First, let's say you're a manager who has just taken over a team. This team is underperforming, and you can pretty quickly tell why. There is a palpable lack of trust, and there are frustrations simmering just barely below the surface, or perhaps right on the surface. People don't collaborate regularly, and when they do you'd almost rather they didn't, because it's far from helpful. Large portions of the team communicate infrequently, and often in coded language, veiled insults, and ways that cover their backsides. And perhaps worst of all, they are either focusing too much on their differences or focusing too much on trying to pretend they're all exactly the same. They're not leveraging their diverse experiences or looking for ways to seek out differentiated points of view.

So, where would you begin? What information would you hope to obtain? How would you go about bringing this collection of individuals together and form a team that strikes the right balance of alignment and strategic misalignment?

Here's another scenario. You've been leading a team for a while. Things are going really well, and everyone knows their role. But the market is changing rapidly, and your team is starting to struggle to keep up. A lack of either skill or will is causing them to fall behind, and it's an unusual feeling for a team that has been used to consistently performing. This is all manifesting differently in different people. Some are starting to hide mistakes or hesitate coming forward to ask for support. Some are collaborating less and focusing more on their own work, to the detriment of team cohesion and varied contributions. Ultimately, the team is losing ground, and it's becoming obvious.

How might you turn this team around and get them back to succeeding? What kinds of conversations would you look to start, and with whom? Can you think about any preliminary behaviors, forms of community, or systems that might be obviously beneficial?

The ABCS are relevant and useful in both of these scenarios. They can help you organize your thoughts, engage people, and deliver stellar results, whether you're repairing a team, building a team, launching a team, or something else related to improving your culture. In all of these cases, the prevailing research and evidence into high performance, regardless of industry or job function, boils down to these four essential ingredients: awareness, behaviors, community, and systems. Following each chapter on the theory behind the ABCS, we'll examine the ideal ways to implement each element, provide examples of what it looks like when it's going well and when it isn't, and then bring them all together in a coherent and simple way.

All of this, of course, is easier said than done. Many of us crave the moments when we can put our paint brushes down, stand back from the masterpiece we've created, and take in the beauty of what we've accomplished. And it's vital that you find moments along the way to appreciate what you and your team have accomplished. In fact, knowing that the work will never be complete for very long doesn't mean that we should avoid celebrating. It means that celebration is even *more* important. Since there is no finish line – only milestones that you set for yourself to track your progress over time – it's crucial that you highlight the moments when a member of your team suggests a non-obvious solution, and you just know that the diversity of the team made that a reality. Recognize the moments of inclusion, when a more extroverted team member recognizes that they've been dominating the conversation, and intentionally takes a step back and leaves room for others to participate and be heard. Recognize when a system makes the desired behavior easier to execute, and the team as a whole benefits. Champion the successes specifically because they are fleeting yet plentiful. They all bundle together to create a track record of optimal performance that makes the journey more fluid, more dynamic, and more likely to achieve success for both the organization and the individuals who comprise it.

Leadership is hard work, but it doesn't have to be complicated. The first step is to start appreciating the value of awareness. So let's start there.

CHAPTER 3

Start with Awareness

Where are you paying attention?

We've all got a lot going on. Working life is full of things to address, and each of those things can be addressed in a seemingly infinite number of ways. What's most important: making your boss happy, job-crafting the role of your dreams, maximizing efficiency, showing up for your employees, playing the political game, or ensuring you're well-liked? Even as we narrow our focus from the limitless number of topics to focus exclusively on people and teams, the possibilities for where to invest our attention can at times seem overwhelming. People from all corners of the organization will make the case that their challenges deserve the highest priority and most immediate attention. While this exercise of prioritization is ultimately up to you, I do want to highlight that two of the biggest risks leaders consistently face are wasting effort by doing the wrong things, and not accounting for the unintended consequences of the actions they take, even when they're doing the right things. Your ability to minimize these risks will put you in the best possible position to gain people's cooperation and sponsorship as you seek to make changes to the organization.

On the first risk, spending time doing the "wrong things" comes with opportunity costs – the energy, time, and resources spent in one place are energy, time, and resources inherently not spent in other places. When we do one thing, we must account for the missed opportunity of the other things we could have been doing. Trying to process so much information and complexity can create a desire to act right away, which can be a clear sign of a bias for action: preferring what's fast over what takes a bit more time and inspection.

When it comes to the second risk, around unintended consequences, it's important to acknowledge that every action creates reactions, ripples throughout the organization. Sometimes those ripples are negligible and have little impact on anyone's experiences at work. But when we're looking at the kinds of changes we're describing, where we are gearing up to change behaviors and systems, it pays to have a degree of confidence in the proposed solution beyond simply guessing. You'll save yourself, and your team, significant time and energy if you can avoid going down false paths, hitting dead ends, and having to reverse course in search of a new solution. Far better to extend your foresight ahead of time, gathering the relevant information from the people who already have a lay of the land both within and outside your company, and charge ahead only when you're ready to do so.

This is what it means to build awareness.

Before making any change, a leader must first know why they're making a particular change and not some other set of changes. The problem is, your view of the world is incomplete. So is mine. Each of our individual experiences and observations alone can't supply us with all the answers to the problems facing groups of people. In some instances, we feel confident that by trusting our gut we'll get things right; and yet, when we really challenge that image of the singular genius, it doesn't hold up to scrutiny. The right teams are almost always better than individuals at problems that require novel thinking or unconventional approaches. You may get lucky from time to time if you choose to forge ahead on your own, but luck alone cannot sustain a business or a team.

Awareness also isn't just about asking the people around us. It's about reading, exploring, watching, and observing, in order to more fully understand an issue and the systems that created and perpetuate it. The goal is to be able to anchor your solution in the foundation of the system. So, you need to go searching for those answers. Awareness is the first step in the ABCS, because there is simply no other way to know what actions you should take to improve how things are done than collecting useful information to build on what you already know, or what you think you already know. Awareness building is the bold act of moving from one shore of ignorant certainty, into the choppy waters of the unknown, hoping it will guide you to enlightenment on the other shore. There is fear in venturing into the waters, but unless you leave your current place of comfort, your situation will never improve.

However, you can't just decide to start learning more about a topic for its own sake. There are just too many things to try to understand at once, and trying to learn everything you can about everything there is won't work. And it's exhausting. A leader from my past used to say, "Don't confuse motion with progress." What he meant was to be deliberate about the difference between doing things for the sake of action, and doing things because they are the right things. Motion is equivalent to wandering aimlessly, hoping to stumble onto an insight or an answer; progress is moving closer to the goal, with intention. Both of these actions require energy. What separates them is that while progress is a worthwhile investment, motion rarely is. It can feel good to do something, anything, in the face of a challenge, but the rush to just do something will soon fade as we are forced to address the same issues again and again. The undisciplined act of building awareness will ultimately prove fruitless because it is not anchored in a business need.

Your goal in this awareness building is not to become more socially conscious or to achieve self-actualization, although those are noble personal goals. Your goal as a leader in an organization is to help your teams increasingly stop doing unproductive things, and more consistently start doing productive things, all with a focus on becoming more effective at achieving the organization's goals. You want to use the information and perspectives you gather to identify which behaviors are the focus of the next step in the process. Any insights you gain during the awareness-building process must be relevant somehow to the problem at hand. Your litmus test is recognizing whether something is merely interesting, or if it's also useful. You can't just have an "aha" moment. You must clearly see how the new information reveals something important about the issue at hand: its incentives, dynamics, relationships, or implications.

Beyond expanding your information on the issue, there are a number of benefits to awareness building. In part, the act of seeking out perspectives, and demonstrating your humility by acknowledging that you don't have all the answers, creates a shared sense of clarity and purpose. People will be able to better understand why this frustrating thing happens, and they can grasp how those mechanisms relate to the work they do. Research has shown this kind of clarity is often highly motivating.[1] When people know the *why* and *how* behind what they're expected to do, they are much more likely to act, rather than wait or freeze. With sufficient reasons to act, and a plan for executing that action, we feel tremendous energy around that action. The only logical next step is to act.

Awareness building, then, is an act of clarification but also one of motivation. By showing people how all the pieces fit together, you're taking a chaotic process and imposing a sense of order. A messy, unreliable story is replaced by a cleaner, more trustworthy one.

This period of time is valuable to you as the leader, and to those around you, as other people begin to join the cause and form the foundation of the work still to come. By asking multiple people for their input, you include them in the decision-making process, building buy-in, and removing yourself as a single point of failure. You can move to the next step of the process, articulating behaviors, with greater confidence and support behind you, rather than assuming that your perspective alone is enough to identify the critical elements. When the people around you know why something is a priority, it increases commitment. On the other hand, when we're guessing and unsure, we're more inclined to avoid action or assume that the need to address something rests with someone else. Leaders who build awareness and share their process and findings with their team, even as working hypotheses, increase the likelihood that people will feel a shared drive to collectively move in the new direction.

A leader who demonstrates the right degree of awareness pays attention to their surroundings, identifying areas of opportunity through qualitative or quantitative data, and staying curious, all up to the time when they need to begin to move beyond inquiry. Many characterize this period of awareness building as the time before you're ready to take action, yet I encourage you to reject that narrative. Building awareness *is* action. The process of building awareness is not passive, and it's not accidental. Building awareness is targeted, intentional, and driven toward establishing the context that will be the foundation for every other step in the ABCS model. Remember, don't confuse motion with progress. Avoid the temptation of thinking that just because you're announcing a major overhaul to a process or policy that you're doing what's best for the company. The best time to figure out where resources should be deployed is *before* you deploy them, not after you've already started. Invest your time and energy in learning where the organization needs the most help, and then make changes. But remember that the awareness building is essential to knowing which changes are the right ones to make.

Awareness building can take a variety of forms. If you're dealing with a situation that resembles something that others have dealt with in the past, or one that comes up often in the ordinary operation of a company, reading about how others have experienced and handled that challenge can be useful. Seek out books and magazine articles that cover a similar topic, or podcasts that feature conversations between leaders who have been in your position. For example, if a company in your industry resolved an improper firing in a way that ultimately seemed to reflect well on that company in the long run, you may use them as a case study and borrow their strategy or tactics if such a situation arises where you work. Perhaps their story was covered in the popular press, or their CEO has discussed the turnaround in a podcast or op-ed column in a business publication. Don't be afraid to borrow great ideas as a starting point, in order to maximize your investment of time. Too many leaders fall into the "not invented here" trap, feeling that their team is so novel and unique that they require bespoke solutions to every challenge, and therefore reject learning from others. This information-gathering period is about learning, not necessarily creating brand new things. It's an act of courage and wisdom, not cowardice or laziness, to learn from leaders who came before you. Take the lessons they learned and apply them so you can get a head start on solving the problems standing before you.

On the other hand, if the challenge truly seems specific to your team or company after you've gone through the search process in books, articles, podcasts, and other media, and you still don't have the answers you're looking for, try collecting perspectives from your colleagues directly. As we've discussed, those colleagues are the ones closest to the action, and they will almost certainly have the clearest sense of what's going on. It can be as straightforward as identifying the relevant stakeholders, any people who are directly affected by the issue, or leaders in the functions at hand, and asking each of them if they wouldn't mind giving you 20–30 minutes of their time. Your goal in these meetings is to uncover how they see the issue, and how it plays out in their corner of the organization, so that you can begin putting some shape to your single point of perspective. While your colleagues may be busy, don't underestimate their willingness to make time for you. Of all the requests you can make of someone's time, I've found asking them to share what their employer could be doing better is seldom a tough ask.

Once you've taken a handful of meetings, the inevitable question that comes up is, *When do I know I'm ready to stop collecting perspectives and move to the next stage?*

Since it's not feasible to speak with everyone in every department, or read everything ever published on a given topic, I find the most reliable indicator that you've heard enough is when you notice an overlap of roughly 80% across the different conversations you're having. That's a good indication that you're beginning to get at the most relevant information. The fact that you'll have collected diverse views is represented in the 20% of each conversation that has been unique and differentiated, and you may find valuable gems in those margins.

Likewise, you'll benefit by remembering that you're only done building awareness for now. You may come back to these folks eventually, as you work through future changes. But the simple act of reiterating to yourself and others that you're done *for now* means that you're acknowledging the need and desire to remain open to new information, yet also the need to move toward action. To paraphrase an old saying, vision without action is daydreaming, and action without vision is a nightmare. Building awareness ensures that you significantly reduce the likelihood that you miss valuable information or embark on the next steps all alone. At the same time, don't be afraid to know when enough is enough. There is a certain amount of trust required in this process – trust in yourself that you performed a good-faith audit of the problem at hand, and trust in others that they were candid and thorough with you. Being afraid to recognize when enough awareness building has taken place can put leaders, and their teams, in the dreaded state of analysis paralysis, where you are hoping for the perfect information to inform the perfect strategy, and that your decisions will be beyond reproach. No decision is beyond reproach, and a crucial part of leadership is being willing to thoughtfully explore uncharted territory, knowing that it's uncharted. In addition to trust, leadership requires an inherent degree of risk and luck, and what awareness building does is reduce the likelihood that risk or luck overwhelms everything you're building.

To bring this to life, let's look at two scenarios, heavily informed by true stories.

In the first scenario, we have a senior leadership team at Company XYZ. Company XYZ is a mid-sized company with operations in a variety of countries, doing business in consumer goods. Leadership has recognized that across the 20,000-person company, women and non-binary employees make up only around 30% of the total population. Given the changing demographics of the company's consumers, the tremendous buying power of women and non-binary customers, and expectations from a wide variety of stakeholders, including current employees, prospective employees, and shareholders, Company XYZ realizes it needs to increase its balance of gender representation.

To do this, there are a number of paths forward. First, Company XYZ can follow what they see others doing in the marketplace. They can copy and paste programs, policies, procedures, and priorities onto their company, and assume that their numbers will begin to mirror their counterparts and competitors, many of whom have greater parity. This approach, though, can be like going to a gym, looking around, and doing the same exercises as everyone else.

While a particular regimen may work for others, it may not work for you. What allowed one company to run a culture program to great success isn't necessarily what will best help Company XYZ, with its unique employee makeup, ways of working, and corporate ambitions.

Alternatively, Company XYZ might take a heavy-handed approach and say that a certain number of roles must be filled by women, or insist that their recruiters start going to different schools or professional associations to find their target audience. The assumption inherent in this approach is that demographics and business outcomes are tied together – that mirroring outcomes in one domain, in terms of female and non-binary headcount, will necessarily mean the company sees the other desired outcomes as well.

Leaders would have valid reasons for pursuing these options, but both are suboptimal because they don't take into account all of the relevant information that lives in employees' heads and all of the relevant forces in Company XYZ's culture that have created a machine where just 30% of staff are female or non-binary. Both options address the surface-level symptoms of the issue, rather than investigating the true underlying issue and its causes.

Instead, think about the benefits Company XYZ leadership enjoys by starting its journey with awareness building. In this case, they may still see what their competitors are doing, yet instead of copying, they are gathering. Simultaneously, they are asking questions. Leadership asks Company XYZ's female and non-binary employees why they chose to work for the company, and why they stay. They ask prospective employees why they applied and what they find interesting about the company. And Company XYZ listens. While they are gathering tremendous amounts of feedback, they realize they won't take on everything, but they are gaining insight into the ecosystem. They're finding out if the challenge is not enough applicants, not the right applicants, a poor screening process, bias in the interview process, inconsistent job offers, a combination of these factors, or something else in the hiring process.

Or they may find that they're hiring at a great rate, and the challenge is actually with retaining female and non-binary employees. Are they leaving soon, not seeing opportunities, not getting mentoring, not having robust development, not getting promoted at a similar rate to their male counterparts, or something else altogether? Again, it may be a collection of challenges, but this stage is about gathering and understanding. It goes beyond assuming the problem is already known and obvious, and having the humility to realize that *new* knowledge must be gathered, and that the only way to create it is through curiosity and active inquisition.

In our second scenario, we have a mid-level manager, Shawn, who is managing teams that split their time between being in the office and working remotely. Shawn has recognized that although he seeks to create an inclusive and creative environment where everyone can contribute, regardless of tenure or hierarchy, he's gotten feedback that certain people are being talked over in meetings, and that it seems to shut down conversation. This is leading to fewer people sharing their ideas, increased tension, and less effective meetings. On top of that, it seems that the people in the office tend to monopolize the conversation compared to people dialing in remotely, and it can be difficult for people on the video platform to contribute.

Shawn can easily institute a policy where anyone who is speaking needs to be able to finish their thought before anyone else can talk. That might solve the immediate challenge, but what else might it create? Might it create group behaviors that seem to value monologues, because even a pause to breathe is seen as an invitation for someone else to start speaking? Might it stifle creativity just as much, because Shawn – the leader – has unilaterally decided that he knows the best path forward?

By embracing awareness as a first step, Shawn instead starts with why. He reads some articles about how to run creative meetings in a hybrid environment. He asks a variety of employees about how the meetings are currently being run, what's working that they'd love to keep, and what they think he might do about the feedback that it can be difficult to participate. Shawn listens to understand, and in doing so, raises the collective awareness of the entire group and begins to build buy-in for what comes next: articulating the specific behaviors that will embody the change.

What these scenarios have in common is a focus on understanding the nature of the issues at hand before trying to solve them. And they're not just any issues. In both scenarios, the relevant issues take into account the goals of the company, whether those are the benefits of diverse and inclusive teams, or effective meetings that capitalize on everyone's contributions. Neither of these scenarios is about prioritizing an issue simply because it happens to be the right thing to do. While that rationale will resonate with some, it will fall flat with others or, worse, lead to protracted disagreements that may drag on for days and distract everyone from the real challenge at hand. Neither of these scenarios involves leaders acknowledging the problem and then trying to ignore it; nor do the leaders put the burden on the communities who are disproportionately affected, and then tell them to just do better. Company XYZ doesn't assume that women just aren't good at interviewing, so Company XYZ would have to "lower the bar" to change their demographics. And Shawn doesn't tell all of the employees that they need to get tough and shout their way into the conversation if they want to be heard. In both scenarios, and in countless scenarios happening in the business world right now, a challenge has presented itself, and it's almost begging to be better understood.

Think about your own team. What challenges have you been facing that just don't seem to go away, no matter how many solutions you've thrown at them? Could the real issue lie in your understanding of the problem? Is there further awareness building that needs to happen in order for the problem to truly be solved? What aren't you seeing? What assumptions are worth revisiting?

In service of building awareness, we've illustrated what it is, why it matters, and what it affords you. So how do you do it? In addition to a strong desire to build awareness, what are the right actions to take? The next chapter will guide you through questions, practices, and examples for how to put awareness into action. Examples of how to engage individuals, groups, people who are peers, more senior, and more junior. These practice chapters will follow each of the theory chapters as you work toward putting the concepts into action.

CHAPTER 4

Awareness Practice

Forget what you "know," ask deep questions, and do your research.

As we just saw, building awareness is the vital first step toward deploying a sustainable solution to a clearly identified problem. To solve the problem, first you have to know what the problem is. Knowing what the problem is can sound easy enough, but in many cases we struggle to identify the problem because we think we already know what's wrong, and we already have the start of an idea for how to fix it. That unintentional confidence can be a major stumbling block toward resolving the issue, because the sense of being right prevents leaders from removing ego, bias, preferences, and preconceived notions from their decision-making process. It's important to be willing to see something in a new and novel way, but that can be incredibly challenging when you've often been rewarded for quickly having the right answers, and lifted up for being able to make decisions quickly.

To be prepared to find the answers, you must accept that you don't already have the answers. To get closer to the root of the problem, you have to go searching.

In this practice chapter and the three practice chapters that come after each element in the ABCS model, you'll find the "Key 3" building actions that bring the model to life. For Awareness, those Key 3 tactics are: *Forget what you "know," Ask deep questions*, and *Do your research*. These tactics are also in sequence, because the order matters. For instance, you shouldn't ask deep questions and do your research, only to forget everything you know. Not helpful.

For Awareness, first you must let go of your preconceptions and adopt a beginner's mindset. Then you need to find people who can give you ideas and insight and ask them good questions. (We'll explore what a "good" question is a little later.) Finally, you need to complement all this with outside research. Exploring the issue internally will give you a great head start. By researching externally, you get the benefit of the wisdom that has come before you, so that you don't need to create solutions all by yourself. Instead, you can use or adapt effective practices that others have tried.

Lastly, alongside each of these building actions is an "eroding action," which helps you identify the most likely trap that may be subtle and disguised, but can very quickly eat away at the progress you're primed to make. The balance of what to do and what to avoid will equip you with the tools you'll need to move ahead with confidence and competence.

Forget What You "Know"
Eroding Action: While there are many things that can undermine your efficacy in the Awareness phase, one of

the most consequential is operating with the belief that you already know exactly what's going on. This perception will lead you to act as if you just need to go through the motions to make other people feel included. It doesn't work.

A sense of overconfidence is an eroding action because it doesn't immediately destroy credibility so much as it spoils things over time, slowly and consistently rotting the inputs and outputs of the work. You'll struggle to pay attention after you ask questions. You'll struggle to show genuine curiosity. Others will notice that you get impatient as they're explaining their point of view. Everything about your demeanor will reveal that you're eager to get to the next phase of the work and may have already made up your mind. That eats at people's desire to share information. It corrodes their contribution and their level of engagement. You can't learn or be taught what you already think you know. That's why the most important thing you can do to forget what you know is to be curious. All good things flow from there. Curiosity is the key because it opens a path toward true learning, by helping you reject anything resembling an ego and its consequences.

In moments of crisis, employees tend to want a decisive, fast-moving expert. When it comes to exiting a burning building, most of us surely want a leader who takes charge, knows the safest way out, and tells everyone exactly what they need to do to survive. But far too often we misjudge problems at work as moments of firefighting when in fact we have plenty of time to take a moment, seek counsel, and then act decisively.

The ability and desire to engage others is a muscle that many leaders need to build. If you notice yourself wanting to skip directly into creating a solution, ask yourself why that is. Do you associate leadership with bold steps and not caring what anyone else thinks? Have you modeled your style on the caricatures that sometimes dominate stories about what good leadership looks or sounds like? Ask yourself why you feel so rushed to get to an answer, and whether bringing others along would allow you to build a solution that is more resilient to challenges, more likely to be adopted, and more likely to solve the problem at hand. Ask yourself what reward you get – whether it's emotional, psychological, or financial – by blazing ahead.

If you find yourself pulled to just take action, reframe your curiosity as a leadership skill and not a weakness or a sign of lacking confidence. Something I like to do when I'm faced with these situations is to reflect on what I would suggest to a trusted friend or peer. If someone came to me with the information that I have, and asked what I'd suggest, I find that I tend to have a solid answer, even if I might struggle to listen to that same advice. Asking what I'd tell a friend is a useful way to force myself to recognize that my suggestion to someone I care about might be different than what I want to do at that moment.

When you feel like you don't have time, energy, or desire to take a step back and force yourself to be curious, think about the alternative and what you might be giving up by charging ahead. By returning to a place of humility and curiosity, you'll be in the right frame of mind to stay open to new information.

Ask Deep Questions

Eroding Action: The classic eroding action to ask deep questions is the temptation to ask leading questions that leave little room for actual insight. Leaders who think they have the right answers, or who lack the patience to properly explore the problem, often ask questions designed to elicit a specific answer. Those may be questions like, "Wouldn't you agree that . . . ?" and "Isn't it true that . . . ?"

These are questions in theory only. They force people into either agreeing with something they may not actually believe, or pushing back on you in a way that may feel uncomfortable to them. Asking leading questions is a way of pretending to invite collaboration, while doing so in a way that ultimately stunts true participation. Avoid this eroding action, and ask deep and genuine questions that provide room for deep and genuine responses.

Once you've embraced a curious mindset, you're ready to ask others for their perspective. This is easier said than done. Most of us have been asking questions since we were toddlers, and yet we're not always good at asking questions in ways that actually uncover new information. This is especially true when we're worried about looking smart or proving ourselves. We may be curious, but our questions need to show that we're curious in a way others can see and feel.

In this regard, we almost always need to start with open questions.

Open questions are those that give the other person an opportunity to explain and expand as they respond. Open questions tend to begin with the classic *Who, What, When, Where, Why,* and *How*. They don't sneak any prior assumptions into their phrasing. They reflect a genuine sense of curiosity on the part of the asker: *Help me understand something I don't currently know.*

Closed questions, meanwhile, are used to confirm understanding and narrow the conversation. Closed questions encourage people to give answers in a more finite space, and can begin with words like *Do, Is, Are,* and *Can*.

Ask yourself: Do you tend to ask more open or closed questions? Neither is inherently right or wrong, but they are appropriate or inappropriate based on what you hope to accomplish. I've met interviewers who struggled to narrow a conversation down because they used nothing but open questions, so the discussion began to meander. And I've experienced conversations that felt borderline painful because the overuse of closed questions elicited terse responses and stunted dialogue.

Look at the following list of open and closed questions and reflect on whether one group feels more natural or right to you. If you recognize that one list sounds much more like you, you may be leaning too heavily on open or closed questions, and you can begin to intentionally add or develop whichever category of questions may feel less natural.

Open Questions
- When did you last experience that?
- What would you like to see us do differently?
- What has been your experience with this topic?
- When was the last time this happened?
- In what ways have you noticed this creating issues?
- Who else would you suggest I speak with?
- What leads you to believe this is an issue?
- How has this affected you?
- Where or when do you find this happens most often?
- What else do you think I should know?

Closed Questions
- Have you noticed others experiencing this also?
- Is it true that people are unhappy?

+ Does our hiring process favor men over women?
+ Are there others sharing similar concerns?
+ Do you think this issue is getting better or worse?
+ How many times have you experienced this in the past month?
+ Did I capture that correctly?
+ Do you find it frustrating when this happens?
+ Was this a helpful conversation?
+ Is there anything else I should know?

The right mix of open and closed questions elicits responses that allow people to get comfortable, open up, share what they have to contribute, and feel validated. In the majority of instances, you'll want to start with open questions in order to gather information. Remember, you're coming into this as a blank slate. The only reason to start with closed questions is to give the conversation a frame, with prompts like, "Do you know why I asked to meet with you?," but if you haven't set up the meeting properly in advance, then even the best questions are not going to get you as far as you'd like. When you've given proper context in advance of the meeting, the other party can come prepared, and open questions are going to be the best way to give them the space to tell you about the issue, in their words.

Once you believe you understand their viewpoint, transitioning to closed questions allows you to confirm your understanding and bring the conversation to an end by asking pointed questions to fill in any of your gaps. As much as questions may seem rudimentary, they are a critical component of the Awareness stage. Great leaders ask great questions.

Do Your Research

Eroding Action: Leaders may be tempted to go back to the same resources over and over to enlighten themselves about a variety of topics, because they feel like those resources hold all the answers. In fact, those resources may supply answers within a much narrower scope than the leader's issues. For instance, leaders may have a favorite thought leader or management guru, and regularly default to that person's perspective as their starting point. In doing so, they may fail to realize that the issue at hand is beyond the guru's expertise, and awkwardly try to fit the guru's solutions to their problems.

By going to the same person or group for all things, you begin to tie your knowledge and success to theirs, thereby lowering your chances of assessing, and therefore solving, the problem correctly.

Once you've asked questions internally and are starting to understand how the problem manifests inside your team or company, the next step is to hear what people are saying about similar challenges outside of your company. When you take a step back from the immediate issue and look at the underlying challenge or concern, it becomes clear that most issues at their core are not completely novel. Sure, times may have changed and the context isn't quite the same, but you can find a wealth of articles, books, and research that will help you digest the knowledge and practices of those who have addressed similar issues.

That's not to say you should take their advice as gospel, but just as you do your due diligence to understand perspectives internally, finding a relevant podcast from a credible source, reading a portion of a book that helps illuminate your thinking, or speaking with a counterpart in another company can be precisely what you need to help round out your information gathering.

As you learn what others have experienced and done, cross-reference what you uncover with what people inside your organization have been telling you. Are you finding significant overlap with what you heard internally and what you're finding externally? Is there new information you might want to consider, which nobody mentioned previously, but feels like it might be an unarticulated need or problem?

Where there is significant overlap between the internal narrative and the external guidance, you can feel confident that the problem you're hearing about is appropriately clear and that you're ready to move ahead, assured that you more fully grasp the issue. Where there is less overlap, and it seems like what you're experiencing is truly novel, you may need to look instead for situations that may be similar while not being exactly the same. Are your employees expressing frustration about an overwhelming amount of change in your organization? Look toward other periods of immense change for inspiration. What did leaders do before, during, and after? How is that relevant to what you're experiencing now?

One of the most important skills you can develop is the ability to spot a problem, see it for its component parts, and recognize places you can turn for information and inspiration. Some people see novelty all around them, but you should be learning to appreciate the unique aspects and still acknowledge the familiar. At its core, the goal of doing your research is similar to the other two of the Key 3, which is to first get out of any echo chamber or information bubble in which you may find yourself. Then, expand your aperture to take in more information before narrowing your focus on the path forward.

I've found a couple of tactics are useful at this stage of the process. The first is to treat this time as if you're preparing to clearly articulate your point of view to someone whose job is to poke holes in your analysis. That means things like keeping a list of your sources, so that if someone challenges your thinking you can point them toward source material. And it means seeking out experts who contradict your emerging point of view, so that you understand the "other sides" of any debate.

The second tactic I rely on is working to silence the inner critic telling me that I'm paid to make these decisions, and that by seeking out the perspectives of others, I'm somehow failing in my role as decision-maker. In reality, that couldn't be further from the truth. My role, and yours, as a leader is to make the best decisions to take care of the team and achieve the goals of the company. When we do that by educating ourselves and getting to better solutions faster, we're doing exactly what we should be. By doing these things you're exposing yourself to new ways of interpreting the world around you, and increasing the likelihood of sustainable success. These are key aspects of a leader's job.

You'll start to feel like you're on the right track with Awareness when you're genuinely excited by learning and gathering insight from others, more than you are fired up by the prospect of relying on your own intuition or expertise. You'll start to feel more like the person who aggregates and synthesizes the world around you, operating by taking in information, more than the person who generates information and pushes it out.

Much of leadership can feel like the world rests on your shoulders and you need to know everything. Awareness building is an opportunity to take a break from that pressure to confidently say that you don't have all the right answers, but you are asking the right questions. You'll have plenty of time in the rest of the ABCS process to be accountable and make hard choices, but for now, learning is better than knowing, and asking is better than telling.

As leaders, sometimes our greatest strength lies in giving other people the chance to tell us what they know. In those moments, our most important jobs are to listen and learn.

CHAPTER 5

Behaviors Over Beliefs

Focus on actions over ideologies.

Imagine you wake up one morning with a mysterious pain that wasn't there the night before. (If you're under 40, this may take some imagination, but when you get to my age, it's kind of a regular thing.) Perhaps in this instance you determine that the discomfort is enough that you need to head to the doctor. When you're with the doctor, you explain the issue, and the doctor attentively and carefully listens, jotting down notes, making great eye contact, and nodding along as you speak. It seems like they may know what's wrong, and you start to hope they have a solution that won't take too much time or cost too much money. And yet, after the doctor is done asking questions, they get up, head to the door, and ask the nurse to walk you to the cashier – no solutions offered.

Wait, what?

Your initial confusion slowly morphs into outrage. What just happened? Well, what happened is the doctor did what leaders do in companies all the time. The doctor asked a bunch of questions, got to some level of

57

understanding, and then carried on with the rest of their day. If the lack of resolution wasn't bad enough, the lack of respect to solve the problem and the wasted time and effort to speak up about it surely is. But such is what corporate teams that are looking to change their culture deal with on a weekly basis.

This is where behaviors come in.

Awareness is about getting to the right nouns and adjectives, being able to understand and explain what is going on, in clear, vivid, and compelling language – the root problem causing pain and discomfort. Awareness is the *who*, *what*, *when*, *where*, and *why*. Behaviors are the verbs. Behaviors are the *how*. They represent the actions that turn mere understanding into a new way of working. Remember, our goal is not to change people's hearts, minds, or beliefs. That's not what work is about. As leaders, our job is to identify where systems and processes are breaking down or could be better, and build behaviors that create more effective, higher-performing cultures.

Identifying the right behaviors after you've gained an awareness of the problem is important to culture change because none of us is working with a bottomless supply of reputation or goodwill. Remember in Chapter 3 when we discussed how clarity is motivating? Well, not doing anything with that motivation is a great way to build resentment. Think of it this way: Accidental ignorance about an issue is bad, because it means you're unaware of what's creating obstacles for your team or your company. Willful ignorance is worse, because it means you know there's an issue, but believe it's easier to look away. Enlightened inaction – that is, taking the time to research the problem, asking others for their opinions and perspective, and then doing nothing – is the worst of all. It means that you as the leader have taken the time to comprehend what's wrong, and now are making an intentional decision to let the problem fester.

In some instances, you may discover that the current situation is better than the alternatives, and in that case it may be appropriate to leave the existing solution in place, akin to leaving a tourniquet on a gash, because removing it may cause more short-term harm to the wound. But the operative phrase there is "short-term." A tourniquet is not a long-term solution, and neither is uncovering an issue, gathering perspectives on options, and then deciding the thing that seemed like such a problem before is actually just fine. Along the same lines, awareness isn't a solution. Awareness is a necessary first step, but it's only the beginning. Awareness building can feel great, because when you do it well, it will give you a newfound sense of clarity and understanding about the nature of the problem at hand. You may be lulled into thinking you've already done the hard part. In reality, you've done *one* of the hard parts. The ABCS challenge us to go far beyond mere awareness building. We have to turn that awareness into new ways of working, otherwise nothing will change. Behaviors are our next step because once you've determined you've gathered enough knowledge along your awareness search, you then have to do something with the knowledge.

Before we get into building the right behaviors, let's take a moment to align on what we mean by behaviors, because not just any behaviors will get the job done.

At the Behaviors stage, it's essential that you can describe as an organization, clearly and succinctly, which new behaviors you believe will help address the problem you're facing. As a manager, you must also be able to explain to your direct reports which behaviors you're going to expect to see from them. In this way, being specific is key. A useful way to judge if you're achieving the right level of specificity is to ask if an outside observer could describe back to you in concrete terms what they see and hear. It's not, "We'll leave some time at the end of every meeting to make sure everyone's been heard," since nobody could tell whether that's actually happening or not. Rather, it's closer to: "When there are 10 minutes left in the meeting, we'll announce it's time to gather people's opinions so everyone feels heard." And even stronger is, "When there are 10 minutes left in the meeting, we'll announce it's time to gather people's opinions so everyone feels heard, and to do that we're going to work in a shared document so that people can add their thoughts all at once, and not feel pressured to contribute." The first one is too vague on both aspects of the behavior, the second is specific around the agenda policy but vague about the implementation, while the third is specific and concrete about both. An outside observer could easily see and hear that a transition is being made, what the purpose of the transition is, and how the final 10 minutes will be spent.

Like the rest of the ABCS model, and work more generally, whether you've reached the right level of specificity in your behaviors is not a binary question, with a simple yes or no. You won't be able to draw a box around the answer like a math problem. Since we're dealing with social situations involving living, breathing human beings, landing on the right behaviors will require some experimentation and flexibility. You may be specific in some ways and still general in others. The goal is to get as specific as possible, without becoming overly rigid. In the earlier example, we specified how the opinions would be captured (i.e. in a shared document), but we didn't specify who owns the document, who's responsible for sharing it to the meeting members, or whose job it is to organize the opinions and send them out as notes after the meeting. (Such details often fall under Systems work, which we'll discuss in later chapters.) In that regard, finding the right level of behaviors is less like flipping a light switch, and more like turning a dial. Each team leader will turn their dial slightly differently depending on the behaviors that best serve the problems elevated in the Awareness stage.

Behaviors also aren't the same as habits in this case. Both are about taking action, but they reflect vastly different priorities and levels of automation.

Habits, such as brushing your teeth or washing your hands, become largely instinctual and unconscious over time. By making these actions automatic, we essentially shrink them into the background of conscious thought, which can free up precious cognitive resources for the more important decisions that come our way. For example, if you've spent the majority of your life washing your hands after you use the restroom or handle something dirty, it just feels like the right thing to do. It becomes habitual because the action itself becomes automated. And that's good, because you don't want to use precious brain power considering whether it's still a good idea to wash your hands this time. And the next time. And the next time. Washing your hands will always be a good idea, and so you embrace that habit to make life more efficient.

Behaviors, by contrast, are intentional and conscious. And for our purposes, turning these new behaviors into habits can actually be counterproductive, because here we *want* to think about what we're doing. We want to pause and reflect on the behaviors. And we want to continue to ask on a semi-regular basis whether those behaviors are continuing to achieve our desired outcomes, or if there's something we should be doing more, less, or differently.

The best habits are ones we can do by thinking as little as possible. The best behaviors are often ones we do by thinking even more than usual.

When workplace behaviors turn into habits, companies and employees lose the intentionality behind the action, which risks allowing the behavior to become yet another company-wide dogma that's followed blindly. This is the birthplace of the dreaded reply to a question about an inefficient process, "Well, we've always done it that way." We want the opposite. We want employees to adopt deliberate behaviors and know exactly why they're doing them.

A final distinction is that while habits are meant to stick with us for a while (sometimes our entire lives, in the case of something like personal hygiene), behaviors are meant to change. Again, that's why the ABCS model is a cycle, not a line. Behaviors are useful only insofar as they still serve the needs established in the Awareness phase. Once we become aware of new problems to solve, and our needs change, the corresponding behaviors have to change as well.

The more specific you can get in articulating the behavior, the better. As we saw earlier, clarity is motivating. Ambiguity makes us freeze. Let's pick up the meeting example again. If instead of being specific and saying that each meeting will include 10 minutes at the end reserved for open discussion in a shared document, we instead just say that the new behavior is to add time at the end of the meeting, people won't know what that means. Some people will wonder if that "space" in each meeting means one minute, five minutes, some percentage of the total meeting time, or something else entirely. With these differing expectations, strife is inevitable. Some people might chime in too early, interrupting the normal agenda, while others will hold back and miss their chance. In a short period of time, the ambiguity will lead to whatever behavior was the norm before to become the norm again. People will default to their past behaviors, thinking to themselves, "Whatever we were doing before feels a lot better than this mess." Change almost never feels great, but add in confusion and it's a recipe for failure.

This idea mirrors what we said before, to avoid confusing motion with progress. If you're training to run a marathon, you can't just go to the gym and toss weights around every day, with the hope you'll get the right kind of fitness to complete your goal. You also can't focus just on running, but only do it once a month and expect to be ready. Making a successful change of any kind is about adopting a clear set of behaviors and executing them along the right cadence. An outsider should be able to look in and observe the new behavior – in the meeting example, by checking their watch to see when the leader of the meeting opens the floor for discussion, hearing any indications that the meeting is turning toward the final item on the agenda, and watching to see how the team members provide their input. If we had 10 observers, each should be able to accurately recount what happened, and there would be consistency across their reports. That would be nearly impossible if the guidance given to each team was to "be inclusive." Being inclusive would mean different things to different people. If there are 10 people in the meeting, it would show up as 10 different behaviors. We want one unifying behavior. While being inclusive may be the ultimate goal, the behaviors themselves are how that goal becomes tangible, shared, and comprehensible.

Perhaps your leadership style or team culture feels more casual than this, and you're thinking, "This is a bit over the top, isn't it?" I invite you to consider whether it's possible that a lack of clarity in some area of the current process is what contributed to the problem you uncovered in the Awareness phase. It may be that in an effort to give people plenty of autonomy, you've actually veered closer toward confusion or disorganization. A bit more structure or specificity than you're used to might invite better outcomes than you expect.

For example, it's often been the case that constraints in certain areas can be useful for driving greater creativity and exploration, by providing useful boundaries. If you asked me to paint a picture (but please don't), I might be overwhelmed with all the ways I could complete that task. *What size should the canvas be? What kind of paint should I use? What's my subject?* And so on. But with just a few parameters – say, a still life of a bowl of fruit, in watercolor – I can deliver on what you want without guessing or hoping I just happen to meet your expectations, and I can still put my own touch of creativity on my work of art.

As a general rule, expectation setting of this kind tends to be underappreciated at work. In an age where so many of us bristle at what can feel like micromanagement, we believe that we'll be better off with unlimited choice and little oversight, and we believe our employees will be better off with greater autonomy as well. The psychologist Barry Schwartz makes a compelling case for the benefits of pruning down some of those options in his book, *The Paradox of Choice*.[1] He observes that some choice is better than none, but it doesn't follow that more choice is necessarily better than some. At a certain point, too much choice becomes paralyzing. At work we often err on the

side of providing tremendous latitude, and don't realize how unclear we're being in our directions, especially
around what good looks like. But if we haven't aligned on
what good looks like, we're all operating from very different places. That miscommunication leads to frustration.

Speaking of frustrations, the Behavior phase may not
always feel so good.

During the Awareness phase, you'll probably start to
sense some consensus. You're gaining alignment on the
issue, and hearing a variety of perspectives that likely
aren't directly at odds with one another. People may disagree about the weight of a factor in causing a given
problem, but they can still see where others are coming
from, and hearing multiple perspectives shouldn't dimin-
ish the value of anyone's point of view. It all feels like
great progress. But going through the Behaviors phase
may feel different. You might experience a bit of a depar-
ture from the consensus you built, as you're forced to
choose among a finite set of behaviors. There might be
friction among the team – especially if they are highly
engaged around the topic – in terms of which courses
of action are most appropriate. In matters related to
the employee experience in particular, we tend to be
quite skilled at the awareness building but offer far too
little clarity about the behaviors we need to implement to
make the right change. There's a kind of holding pattern,
where people know there's something to be done but
there's little to no consensus on what needs to happen
now. This is the place where people may lose interest
and disengage, or lose patience and lash out, because
they believe in the priority but not the solution.

For this reason, velocity matters. Velocity is defined
as both direction and speed. You might have one or the
other, but we need both to achieve our goals. Going in

the right direction, but moving so slowly that progress is imperceptible, isn't good enough. Going quickly, and in the wrong direction, is a fool's errand. We need to be going the right way, with the right speed, to add value and start bringing people together.

This is a period where the best practices of change management come in handy – that is, giving people the context for a decision and communicating your thought process so that people can respect and understand, even if they don't necessarily agree with the outcome. Two elements of any good change management strategy are establishing the need for the change, and painting a clear picture of the future state. Since there are a multitude of feasible solutions in any scenario, you have to prune those down to the select handful of behaviors that you can articulate clearly and scale to the wider team or organization. More on specific change management practices in the next chapter.

One of the most important aspects of this Behaviors phase is being clear that you don't believe you've identified all of the right behaviors, but instead that you've identified *some* of the key behaviors. The goal is to identify the behaviors that provide the greatest leverage against the challenge at hand. While there may be disagreement about the behaviors you select, your barometer of success is not agreement; it's clarity. If you gauge the readiness to move ahead by whether everyone is aligned and in full agreement that these are the right behaviors, and the only behaviors worth adopting, you will be waiting a long time. And the larger the group, the harder it will be to reach anything nearing consensus.

Success is not about achieving perfection on the first pass. It's about progress – at first usually in big leaps, and over time in smaller steps of refinement. Doing that requires careful testing, with the recognition that a measure of grace is necessary for getting things wrong and making mistakes. You and your teammates are making good-faith efforts to change your culture for the better. Don't let perfection become the enemy of progress.

Once you've established the right behaviors, communicated them to the right initial audience, and begun implementing the behaviors, you need to make those behaviors stick, and prevent the wrong behaviors from leaking in. To give people a good experience with the changes, I recommend limiting the number of new behaviors to just a few. Trying to do too many things revolving around the same topic at once can be overwhelming and can lead people to reject the whole change. For instance, imagine trying to give up caffeine, sugar, and alcohol all at once. It's feasible, but exponentially more challenging than giving up just one of the three, and even more so if the change is someone else's idea rather than your own. Likewise, as much as this problem you've identified and researched is salient to you, there are likely other changes happening in other parts of the business, which may affect the same people you're trying to impact. When you identify as few behaviors as possible, while still keeping the change central to the efforts, you show that you understand what you're asking of others and that you acknowledge the limits of their resources. And while the challenges may lend themselves to a single set of behaviors for all parties, it may be the case that there are people along different stages of the problem, who have different actions to take. For instance, if you identified issues with your hiring process as the culprit, you may have a behavior for the recruiter, a behavior for the interview panel, a behavior for the hiring manager, and a behavior for the onboarding team. Each of these are in support of remedying the issue at hand.

Keeping with our example of leaving 10 minutes for everyone to contribute their ideas at the end of the meeting, the first few times you do it will seem odd and clunky. After a while the behavior will start to become more natural, and people will see opportunities for enhancement. Reject this impulse for a bit, and just get the rhythm down first. Keep a log of people's suggestions for implementation when the time is right, but the time to start innovating is not while the behaviors are still new. Behaviors are going to evolve as the organization evolves, but for now these are the right behaviors.

To see this in action, let's check in on a leader named Preeti. It's been brought to Preeti's attention that her global team is struggling with picking meeting times that work for everyone, even more so given the flexibility she and her team have prioritized when it relates to working schedules. Preeti understands that some of her employees are parents, some have hobbies, and still others have different working preferences related to when they feel like they're able to do their best work. The mix of early birds, night owls, and those who are at their peak midday, is proving challenging for getting collaborative work done. Preeti has worked through the Awareness stage and identified the problems. She's done her homework in asking, reading, and listening, to fully ensure that she understands not just the surface-level symptoms of the challenges, but what may be the underlying issues that are creating the environment where this confusion has become the norm – for example, the emerging sense of entitlement that no one should have to adjust their schedule to meet the broader needs of the team. Preeti has asked tough questions, and gotten to a place where she feels comfortable that she can, and should, move on toward solutions. So, we find her at the Behaviors stage. Preeti partners with her small circle of diverse views to work through what might be a realistic and productive change. And she is clear that they're working through what *might* work, because the only guarantee is that Preeti and her team are going to work hard, learn, and adjust.

Preeti and her collaborators don't stop at the broad strokes of language, which can be where so many other leaders begin and end. The less intentional leader can often make the mistake of dealing in generalities and vagueness. But in this instance, Preeti and her team do the work and push themselves to clarify what the behaviors are, how to explain the behaviors in simple terms, and how to know whether the behaviors are actually happening or not. Far from assuming that "people are smart and will just get it," they know that even smart people benefit from clarity, and that if this problem were going to solve itself, it would have been solved by now. And far from assuming that "people are dumb, and we need to explain it," they know that precision in their guidance is not a lack of respect for their co-workers. Preeti and her team know that everyone around them is engaged in other tasks, absorbing a lot of information, pulled in a variety of directions – both inside and outside of work – and that if Preeti and team have any hope of changing behaviors, those behaviors need to be clear and concise. Based on what Preeti and her team have researched and discussed, that might sound like alignment around a four-hour block each day from Monday through Thursday, when all members of the team are expected to make themselves available for collaboration and meetings, along with alignment around how the team communicates asynchronously during other times. These behaviors pass the filter of whether an observer could see or hear them, because we could look at calendars and see if team members are creating space for collaboration during the times Preeti and her team have designated. This team has gone beyond where other teams might stop, with the platitude to "prioritize collaboration." That path forward with thoughtful clarity is a sign of their care for the importance of the work, and their very real limits along with the limits of the people around them. And now that Preeti and her team have completed these two stages, they're ready to move on to sharing what they've learned, and generating energy around what comes next.

At this point we've identified what matters, gotten clear on how we're going to address it, and we're well on our way to creating a higher-performing culture. In the next chapter, we'll look at specific ways to craft the behaviors that solve your problems and move you even closer to the culture you want to build.

CHAPTER 6

Behaviors Practice

Be specific, use plain language, and make it shareable.

Once you've identified the issue at hand – the problem that has been discovered and described – you may find yourself getting excited about overcoming this first obstacle. You may have a rush of excitement about having figured out this challenge that is sapping efficiency from the team and getting in the way of achieving your goals. That burst of energy is a good thing – akin to reaching a key milestone like finishing putting together the border on a jigsaw puzzle. And just like a physical puzzle, this organizational puzzle you're working on isn't done when you reach that milestone. There is more work to do, and the picture, literal or figurative, is incomplete. Take the energy and use it to propel you to this next stage of the ABCS cycle.

While you're harnessing that energy, it's crucial not to lose focus, because this is the point where you'll start working on describing the proposed behaviors at the right level of specificity, simplicity, and shareability. Nailing all three priorities is one of the most difficult aspects of the ABCS work. It's difficult in part because behaviors are how real changes start to happen, and what's more, not just any articulation will be enough to achieve the desired outcomes. This practice chapter focuses on how to articulate the right behaviors in the right way.

What we're fighting against is ambiguity in what people should do, and against behaviors that are unreasonably challenging. If the behaviors are too vague or too hard, you're putting yourself and your team at a disadvantage from the very start. To put it another way, this work is like cooking an important meal for a big group; being too vague at this step is like trying to prepare all of the dishes without clear recipes, and being too challenging at this step is like starting the meal with Beef Wellington and ending with Baked Alaska. By the very nature of what we're doing, there will be effort involved, but getting the behaviors right means that the effort is as efficient as possible. Our goal is no wasted effort.

Lastly, while we're building the right behaviors, we also want to build the description of these behaviors in ways that make them easy to share with others, as we look toward building community, the next stage of the ABCS model.

With those guiding priorities in mind, the Key 3 for your Behaviors practice are: *Be specific, Use plain language,* and *Make it shareable.* Let's take a closer look at each one.

Be Specific

Eroding Action: In many cases, leaders may believe that being specific is a sign of disrespect for the autonomy and intelligence of their employees and co-workers. They can trick themselves into believing that by providing only high-level guidance, they are demonstrating a visionary leadership style and giving their employees just enough of the necessary context for a certain task. As such, they can be confident that they are providing employees the latitude and creativity to find whatever path toward a solution works best for each individual. In reality, the leader is usually just being unclear. That lack of clarity, while perhaps meant with the best intention to allow deference to others, can unintentionally cause more frustration and confusion, which are sure to lead to more strife and wasted effort.

Likewise, leaders sometimes believe that if the people around them are smart and capable, then articulating specific behaviors can feel like treating those employees like children or disrespecting their expertise. No good leader wants to micromanage others, and in an effort to avoid demonstrating one type of poor leadership, leaders can accidentally demonstrate another type of poor leadership. In my experience, micromanagement has far less to do with aligning around shared problems and solutions, than it does with telling people how to do every aspect of their job. Clarity and alignment are not the same as micromanagement. By providing clear and unambiguous guidance, your team will be far better equipped to deliver on the desired behaviors, without your constant attention, observation, and intervention.

Another reason leaders sometimes avoid specific language is that they may have the thought, "If I need to describe this level of detail, then we have the wrong people." That's not true. The people on your team are likely busy, cognitively taxed, pulled in many directions, and working hard to deliver on the company's objectives. Smart and capable people like to know what the team is aligning around, so that they can perform the desired actions. Instead of viewing clarity as an obstacle, the strongest cultures see clarity as useful and healthy, not as leadership overreach.

As we explored in the last chapter, the first priority when crafting behaviors is to identify the right action in vivid, observable language. One of the easiest tests is to ask yourself whether you or someone else could record the behaviors. It would be impossible to record "Be more inclusive," "Listen actively," or "Be respectful." While all of those are great general pieces of advice and ways of working, they lack the crucial quality of being specific enough to organize our actions around. Each person will interpret these general phrases differently, and that inconsistency will lead to disunity and disorganization.

Specificity matters because this is where the proverbial rubber meets the road in terms of bringing the solution to life. Up to this point you've clarified the problem, but a problem without a useful solution isn't the goal. If the words capturing the change aren't specific enough, then the change can't go far enough.

In some sense, the words help facilitate the change. Shakespeare famously wrote "What's in a name? That which we call a rose, by any other word would smell as sweet," suggesting that words and the objects they represent aren't necessarily connected. And with all due respect to Mr. Shakespeare, in this case the words do matter. To make this more concrete, here are some examples of non-specific behaviors, and how we might improve them.

Instead of:
♦ Giving better feedback
♦ Helping your teammates
♦ Putting the customer first
♦ Being on time

Try:

- ◆ Telling the other person the action, and what you believe was the impact
- ◆ Asking a teammate, "What can I help you with?"
- ◆ Greeting customers within 60 seconds and give your name and an offer of assistance
- ◆ Arriving between two and five minutes early for every meeting

When we're general or abstract, we leave room for misunderstanding. When we're specific and concrete, we describe things and events in the real world that we can all observe. Articulating the change we want to see at this level of resolution is how we ensure that change actually happens.

Use Plain Language

Eroding Action: In a plethora of instances, executives with a propensity for obtuse rhetoric and incoherent articulations obscure their intentions by prioritizing wit over comprehensibility.

Did that sentence make sense to you the first time you read it? Did you bother to go back and read it again?

To say that same thing in another way, I can say that leaders often use big words to get their point across, and put sounding smart over communicating well. They believe it projects intelligence and seriousness. Do everything you can to avoid being that person. Sometimes you will naturally fall into using abbreviations and internal language because it's a way to show that you're an insider and can communicate in the language everyone else is using. But remember that using acronyms and big words when plain language will do is partly why the corporate world gets such a bad reputation as stuffy and out of touch. It can also be why new employees struggle to comprehend what's being said, and why people can feel like outsiders for far too long. At best this kind of communication is mocked; at worst it creates confusion that prevents important work from getting done.

An over-reliance on projecting intellect can also build barriers between those who have been around the company for a while and have learned the lingo, and those who may be new and are struggling to keep up. This is especially true when leaders use idioms, metaphors, and turns of phrase that might not translate across audiences and cultures. In a workplace where many of your partners likely come from different backgrounds, points of view, and generations, jargon doesn't work because no one really understands what they're supposed to do.

In his writing manual *The Sense of Style*, cognitive scientist Steven Pinker explains how self-consciousness can contribute to poor communication. Academic writing and legal documents, for instance, are full of unnecessarily large words and complicated sentence structures, presumably to seem more sophisticated.[1] But before we point the finger to laugh at or judge academia and law, remember that corporate speak is all-too-often guilty of similar offenses. Even though our human brains are wired to think in pictures and patterns, our egos can get in the way and steer us to speak and write in complicated language detached from reality.[2] We have to resist this temptation. The only thing more important than the message itself may be how we convey it. With so many modern and complex demands on our time, energy, and attention, simplicity is one of your biggest advantages.

Plain language is different from the first Key 3 in the Behaviors practice, *Be Specific*. It's quite possible that in an effort to be specific, a practitioner of the ABCS may use more words and greater complexity as a substitute for being specific. For example, if you want to create a behavior to address inconsistent interviewing practices, the behavior *Systematize and standardize question-asking* is arguably specific but poorly worded. Likewise, it's plain but not concrete to say, *Ask everyone the same questions.* (Which questions, and in which order?) A more specific behavior in plain language might be, *Follow the applicant interview guide.* Far too often we mistake fancy and confusing talk for intelligence, yet the smartest thing you can do is to make sure you are communicating with an end goal of being understood.

Instead of:

- Quantifying the client impact, to maximize their engagement
- Capitalizing on the low-hanging fruit
- Embracing blue-sky thinking
- Identifying synergies and leverage the team's core competencies

Try:

- Sharing the benefit to the client in two to three key data points
- Capturing the top three actions that will require the least effort
- Taking five minutes in the monthly meeting and write down your ideas for future products and services
- Using the weekly call to find one to two actions where one team member can support another

By avoiding the pull toward complexity, we increase the likelihood of understanding, which is key to any culture change. The best designers, whether they are architects, engineers, artists, or technologists, know that the greatest success is to take something complex and make it seem so simple as to be almost self-evident. A few brush strokes by Pablo Picasso. A simple sentence by Mark Twain. A fluid user interface by your favorite tech company. All of these examples reflect a directive often attributed to Albert Einstein: Make a thing as simple as possible, but no simpler.

Make It Shareable

Eroding Action: Leaders tend to think too narrowly around who will need to understand the behaviors. Language can be specific and plain, but not engaging or interesting. If the language isn't easy to share, then it will suffer from a communication challenge. It's very possible to get caught in the trap of creating behaviors just for your immediate team or department, without thinking ahead to how the behaviors might scale. It may all begin in your closest circle of influence, since that's where you have the greatest visibility and the most control, but in an ideal scenario you're creating behaviors that will resonate with those outside of your closest partners.

If you don't think about how the people around you will share the behaviors with others, you're inherently limiting your influence and capacity to effect broader change.

Once you have made the behaviors specific and captured them in plain language, you can think about how to adjust them ever so slightly, so that they're easier to share. This is where things like rhyming, alliteration, and leveraging existing connections, such as internal workplace memes, are powerful.

These communication tools make language easier to share by making it more "fluent." Our brains have an easier time processing this familiar language and its meaning than if it were phrased differently. Some research even suggests that fluent statements feel truer than disfluent ones, such as the phrase "woes unite foes" versus "woes unite enemies."[3] As you craft new behaviors, increased fluency can reduce friction by making the language easier to understand, easier to internalize, and ultimately easier to share.

The trick at this point is to add fluency without sacrificing the clarity and plainness that you've already established. Many corporate initiatives fail not simply because they're overly complicated, but also because leaders get too caught up in making them catchy or clever and losing sight of simple and plain. Never let being clever come at the expense of being clear.

Instead of:
- Maximizing the time spent in meetings by getting clear on decisions and actions
- Reducing the complexity of each meeting by focusing on fewer things
- Starting every email with the most important information, to ensure the recipient understands what is expected of them

Try:
- Making meetings matter. Capture meeting minutes and actions, and share within 24 hours
- Having no more than three topics, and two actions, in one meeting
- Beginning every email with the action, information, or request (AIR)

One of the biggest challenges with the Behaviors stage of the ABCS model is striking the right balance among the Key 3. You can think of the ideal behaviors as those that live at the intersection of a three-way Venn diagram (Figure 6.1).

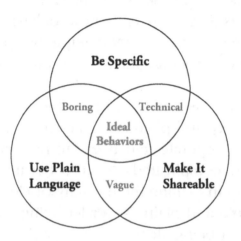

Figure 6.1 Use this Venn diagram to create the ideal behaviors that people understand, can use in their everyday work, and feel compelled to share.

It's possible to have none, one, two, or all three of the Key 3. In the best-case scenario, the behaviors you describe will achieve all three, but that may not always be the case. Let's listen in to some things you might overhear when you're missing one or two of the Key 3.

Specific only: *"This is a lot of words to describe this behavior. It's like listening to someone read an instruction manual."*

Plain language only: *"I love that we're finally ditching all the acronyms, and speaking like normal people do, but what are we actually supposed to do?"*

Shareable only: *"That is really witty and pretty catchy, but I'm not clear on the action. Are you?"*

Specific and plain, but not shareable: *"Ah, I get it! I'm not sure if it'll be easy for others to remember, but we can try."*

Specific and shareable, but not plain: *"This probably only makes sense to us . . . but it does make sense to us!"*

Plain and shareable, but not specific: *"Cool slogan, but a bit light on the details"*

You may find it challenging to situate the behavior you need to describe at the intersection of these Key 3. If you need to sacrifice one, let it be *Make it shareable.* What you lose in a shareable message, you can make up by showing your successes and leveraging your network to get the message out. It will be more challenging, but if you forgo specificity, you invite ambiguity, and if you forgo plainness, you invite unnecessary complexity. Making it shareable primes you for going broader, but if you don't get the first two elements right, then sharing it broadly is actually a bad idea, because you'll just spread the confusion and complexity. But when you get this right, the behaviors people are most likely to carry out on a repeat basis are the ones that are easy to understand, easy to say, and easy to share. Hit all three, and you've got a great shot at changing your culture as quickly and sustainably as possible.

CHAPTER 7

Cultivating Community

Be a good neighbor to your colleagues.

At this point, you've worked through the deep listening and information gathering that are some of the hallmarks of building awareness. You've also clearly defined the desired behaviors to the degree that you can expect a reasonable employee to understand and demonstrate those behaviors. Altogether, you've primed a small group of employees with the education, instruction, and presumably the passion to implement an important change.

So how do you send all of that good work rippling outward into a broader group, like a stone dropped into a pond?

The answer is the next step in ABCS: Community.

The Community step of the cycle reflects the need to socialize the culture change to people who weren't necessarily within the core group of instigators. Those who have been along for the journey are far more likely to understand the need, see how the articulated behaviors help address that need, and be ready to engage to solve the problem at hand.

It's not a guarantee that everyone who has been engaged will agree with the need, or believe that the behaviors you're testing are the right or complete behaviors. But when comparing those who have advanced notice and participation in a process with those who are learning about all of this at this stage, there's usually a noticeable difference in their receptivity, and of course in their comprehension. When you've opened yourself to exploring the right problems in the Awareness phase, and the behaviors to address those problems make sense in an objective way, it should feel rather obvious to those being engaged at this point why this matters. They'll be more likely to hear about the suggested improvements and react with curiosity and perhaps even a sentiment such as, "I get it. It makes sense. I've noticed that in my work, too."

There will certainly be times when a problem is exposed to only a few people, or some people are impacted by an issue but are unaware of what's actually causing it. In this case, they might be unaware of how this change will help benefit them, but part of your responsibility is to illuminate at the Community stage what's in it for them. Like every great change management model over the past few decades, you must build a "pull" that draws people in, instead of relying on a "push" that forces them to change their ways. Nobody does anything unless it feels like the right thing to do, for them. Even if the people you're hoping to bring along see the logic in your actions, if it doesn't feel right, they won't feel the pull to make a change. They will feel pushed, and so they will resist. Your goal is to make it clear how the change meets their needs as well as their wants. If you can make the needs seem like wants, even better.

Still, there will be detractors and laggards throughout this process. There will be people for whom the effort feels annoying or painful enough that the current state seems just fine. For every group of employees who are thrilled that they may now be able to speak up in a meeting or contribute their ideas without having to yell over the crowd, there will be employees who are bitter that they don't get as much speaking time now, because the old way benefitted their style or efforts. Trying to win over every employee is unrealistic, much like in our Awareness stage when we talked about trying to learn all of the information. Beyond a point, the effort to bring more people to a place of acceptance is effort that can be better spent deploying, measuring, and iterating. We must choose our opportunity costs wisely. There are costs to not doing enough, but there are also costs to doing too much, at the expense of other things that are potentially more valuable to your overall efforts.

That said, if enough people react skeptically, wondering aloud with comments like, "Where is this coming from?" you may have unintentionally created a solution in search of a problem. The problem you're addressing might be a phantom problem, or it might just be a minor nuisance to a small group of people. If that's the case, then you may need to do some additional awareness building to understand the scope of the problem in finer detail, or the size of the community you're looking to engage may be narrower than you anticipated, and you may need to shrink your solution to target just that group.

Over the course of any relationship, whether with friends, partners, neighbors, or at work, there will be disagreement about a path forward. In each situation we need to decide if our disagreement is so principled or ferocious that we simply cannot participate – in which case, we need to explore changing the decision, changing ourselves, or leaving. But when the decision is made, we need to be prepared to expect our team to help deliver that decision as if it was their own. Or, as leadership at one of my past employers was fond of saying, "Disagree, and then commit."

Through these disagreements, we are continuing to define what work is, and what work isn't. The essence of the ABCS cycle is that we're doing our best to identify the challenges and deploy behaviors that will maximize the benefit, minimize the unintended consequences, and then learn, learn, learn. In the end, if you have broad consensus but a few vocal challengers, it may be necessary to concede the two sides disagree, but for the sake of the group, ask that the opposing viewpoints commit to the change anyway.

Your role in community building varies depending on your place in the leadership hierarchy. If you're an executive or senior leader, your role likely involves using your influence to enact broad and sweeping change. The higher you go, the more your influence cascades throughout the organization. The CEO, for instance, has the scope and responsibility to know which issues are the biggest ones facing the company, before collecting the right people to understand how to solve those issues and enacting changes – policy and otherwise – to move the organization forward. This can sometimes happen with a single proclamation, but that's seldom the best path forward. The better path forward involves building a coalition among a company's managers and supervisors, who are embedded deeper in the company and tend to have a more grassroots path to effecting change, especially in a large organization.

Community building at the level of middle management involves sharing and learning with the groups, partners, collaborators, and peers in their closest proximity. It's less about imposing change, and more about showing what works through proof and examples so that people across the organization see value in doing the new thing instead of the old thing.

In any case, you'll know the community building is along the right path when you begin to see and hear the right behaviors, even when the leader who initiated the change isn't around. When the change depends on the right person being in the room, any progress is inherently temporary. When people only do something when someone else is looking, it's not commitment. It's compliance. And since the very nature of this work is iterative, we're looking for commitment to wholehearted experimentation, not blind obedience. The act of embedding the change is reinforced in the Systems stage of ABCS, but it begins here, at Community. If the behaviors live with a single person, the behaviors leave with a single person. The sign of a good leader and a strong culture is what happens when you're not around.

In the Behaviors chapter we saw how implementing new actions is an inflection point that moves an important change from an idea in people's heads to a set of actions that make a real-world impact. Community is another inflection point. In this case, Community is what helps scale a local impact into something broader and more capable of widespread change. It's how you can amplify a behavior from an individual to a team, and then to a whole division or company.

Your ability, or inability, to build a sense of community around the problem and corresponding behaviors is an element of what determines if the progress is local and targeted, or widespread and expansive. This creates a need for another set of skills that are often underutilized, and that's understanding how much change your team can truly tolerate. I've heard leaders refer to this as the "gulp rate." How much can your team consume before it becomes overwhelming? Every team has a natural appetite and capacity for change, and while I've never seen a metric or rubric that can measure this, I've seen leaders who are emotionally aware enough to know when their teams are reaching that crucial point. I've also seen leaders who pushed beyond it, and suffered the consequences of a team that dropped it all, like a server bringing out too many platters at once. When it all comes crashing down, it's a mess to clean up.

Again, this pursuit is anchored in the mantra "progress over perfection." The drive to create perfect behaviors among the entire team or department creates an unhelpful pressure. Experimentation and learning are part of the cycle, not something to be avoided. True, there are principles that make some behaviors more effective than others, but don't fall into the trap of thinking the behavior has to be perfect. Instead, embrace the feedback loop. Decide whether the proposed behavior meets a reasonable set of criteria, and then implement them. Soon enough you'll start to hear what's working and what's not. During this process, you must let the new behaviors settle. Give them time to work. Don't try to reinvent the behaviors from week to week just for the sake of novelty, or because they don't seem to be working yet, or because you're uncomfortable sitting with something new. Trust the community you're building to let the feedback loop work as intended.

In smaller companies that loop can be quite quick; the signal goes out and comes back without much delay. You can be there to see some of the changes, the looks on people's faces, the degree to which the behaviors are being embraced or rejected. In larger companies it can be more challenging to wait for that return signal carrying word of how things are going. Larger companies can suffer from something akin to a whiplash effect, where the changes may be small at the place where the action is initiated, and yet by the time it goes through layers, the effect can be amplified and exaggerated.

The size of the organization, however, is not the sole determining factor in the speed of the signal. Companies can be big and fast, or small and slow. What matters more is how quickly word of the new behaviors can permeate the intended group. How quickly can the behavior spread? In a nimble company, large or small, we're talking about the equivalent of employees receiving a text message – word gets around quickly. In a sluggish company, large or small, we're talking about the equivalent of carrier pigeons – other information gets in the way, delaying receipt of the message and its effectiveness.

By the time the message makes its way back to you, as the leader of the change, some degree of reworking has probably already happened, because each group will personalize the new change in slight yet important ways. And all of this is just one problem and set of behaviors at a time. Often there are multiple signals going out and coming back. Unlike a lab, where researchers can isolate a single variable and identify the unique impact of changing that one thing, it will be difficult with so many simultaneous efforts to know exactly what is affecting what other elements.

This gets back to our gulp rate. Anything that stresses the system too much risks creating disengagement. Just as a good stretch for the body can be healthy and productive, too much of a stretch can pull or tear something and require healing time, there comes a point where a team's stretch becomes a tear, and an unattended tear can have negative overall health impacts, including delays in the culture change effort. Since the community you're seeking to engage hasn't been part of the core change effort, they likely only have so much energy they're willing to invest, after which they'll do whatever is easier or avoids them getting in trouble. Calibrate the scale of the change accordingly. If it feels like there are too many new behaviors cycling through at once, work with your team to identify the one or two behaviors that represent the lowest priorities and could be temporarily paused if needed. You can revisit implementing those behaviors once the other behaviors have settled into the normal ways of working.

Now that we've explored how community building works within an organization, it may be a good time to reflect on the idea of the workplace as a community. The metaphor doesn't stretch into infinity, but for our purposes it does help to think of our shared responsibilities and accountabilities as similar to people who live near each other.

First off, notice I didn't say "families." Healthy company cultures aren't families. I've never met a family that downsized because of a bad product launch, or paid each other to come to family events. Teams are more like neighbors who have their own responsibilities, obligations, and expectations, and yet they are governed by an overarching set of rules that bind them together. What one neighbor does affects the others, sometimes to a large degree.

The degree to which your neighbor affects you, or not, can extend our metaphor to help explain the difference between a neighborhood and a commune.

In a neighborhood, you each have your own space, your own responsibilities, and are accountable for the decisions you make. While the condition of your household may tangentially affect others, there's still a degree of separation and distance, both physical and psychological, that defines a neighborhood. The relationships that bring you together and the tensions that pull you apart are found largely in the common spaces and when your worlds overlap. By contrast, a commune is defined by the overlap. It's an environment in which the actions of one have a tangible impact on others. There's less room for separation, less opportunity for isolation, and more reliance and interconnectivity.

At work, there may be groups over which you don't have direct authority, but whose actions directly affect your ability to get things done. They are a part of your commune. There are others with whom you work in a similar space, but you could change the way you operate, and they would be largely unaffected, and might not even know; those are your neighbors. At work you chat, meet, collaborate, and generally look out for each other. When there are shared goals, whether in your community or at work, you come together to accomplish things that would be challenging to accomplish individually.

In this way, each team in the company is like each household in the community. The behaviors that seem so routine and normal in your context may not work in another.

For instance, let's say you have a rule in your home that prohibits technology at the dinner table. As you invite others to your home, you may tell them about your rule, and ask them to participate. As you go to their home, you would likely leave your rule at home, because you're in someone else's space. But if you were to find that your neighbor complained about the lack of conversation at dinner because their partner or roommates were on their phone all the time, you might tell them about the behavior you've implemented, the problem it was meant to solve, and how it's working. This is one of the benefits of being so clear about what challenge you're solving, through awareness, and how you're solving it, through behaviors, because when someone shares a similar challenge you can be a part of *their* awareness building, as you provide insight into what you've done and what you've learned.

Creating widespread behavior change many times comes down to this kind of information sharing, and knowing the appropriate time to share what's working for you, because their problems match ones that you're solving, and knowing when to ask others what's working for them, because their solutions may help you.

Thinking about community building at work through the metaphor of community building in general can be a useful lens, because it helps us appreciate that there's no single solution to everyone's challenges.

Say, for instance, that we now check in on Jon, a leader who recognizes through feedback and observation that one of his team's biggest issues is a lack of critical feedback. People have gotten too comfortable and polite, leading to an ineffective culture of niceness. Jon has heard about the issue of being overly cordial, raised the awareness by asking questions and reviewing materials to help round out the group's perspective, established specific behaviors targeted at increasing candid feedback, and things are starting to work well for the group.

In this instance, the appropriate behavior Jon and his team adopted was to appoint someone to help present a dissenting viewpoint, which role models the desired behavior and encourages everyone else to probe and dissent productively. Jon is getting good feedback from the team, not seeing any negative reactions to the new behavior, and the results are self-evident; the team is putting out better solutions and the team meetings are more dynamic and engaging. Well done Jon and team!

However, if Jon's team were to attend a larger group meeting led by another team, they likely wouldn't bring this behavior to that meeting, since without the right context it might seem rude and disruptive. As a participant in someone else's meeting, the respectful thing to do is to recognize that this other group may have behaviors that work for their culture. And if someone else were to attend Jon's meeting, and saw someone constantly disagreeing with the group's discussion, they might be taken aback if Jon or someone else hadn't explained to them that this is how this team's meetings run.

This is where recognizing that different teams have different challenges, and different challenges require different behaviors, is a new way of understanding the cultures around us. In this case, Jon wouldn't expect someone to tell him that his way of running his meetings is "wrong," nor would Jon realistically expect to impose his meeting style on another leader. By approaching the situation with curiosity instead of judgment, others can see that this behavior of the person modeling candid and constructive feedback can be appropriate for addressing a lack of energy or appropriate conflict in meetings. That seed has been planted, and if Jon or someone familiar with this behavior runs into a similar issue on a different team, or hears another leader express concern that it's happening on their team, they have an example of a behavior that can be deployed, if suitable.

This is akin to a community where one neighbor has a new lawn care routine or found an amazing new person to call for repairs. They wouldn't necessarily push their solutions on others unsolicited, but in a strong community they would certainly make the information available if they knew someone was struggling with weeds or had a leaky faucet.

One way to gain a broader perspective of what others are doing is simply to ask if you can attend a meeting and observe. Think of it as the modern version of "management by walking around," in which you get to see what's working on another team and what you can add to your repertoire. You'll start to see different behaviors that are grounded in different challenges, with robust awareness behind them, and so what you see and hear may pleasantly surprise you. Meetings are often the window to the company. While top-down initiatives will almost always have their place, groundswell change is equally, if not more, important. Keeping your eyes and ears open for what's working, and asking what the initiatives are solving for, is an important practice, and perhaps might even become one of your organizational behaviors. Asking about the problems that the behaviors solve is important, because you may see things that at first seem odd, but in context seem brilliant. Alternatively, you may see things that seem self-evident, but provide you much more insight when you understand the reason why that behavior came to be. In turn, if you've heard or seen a fellow leader potentially struggling with an issue your team has solved or dealt with in the past, invite them to one of your meetings so they can see the solution for themselves. This is what it looks like to create a sense of community around shared goals and interests.

As you work through the ABCS model, what you're likely to see is that the frame of the world in which you operate has gotten a bit larger. Instead of focusing exclusively on those in your closest proximity in terms of daily activities and work, you will almost inevitably start to branch out and bring to others the insights you've gained and the behaviors you're employing. You will begin to see the seeds of change in your own team take root, and in many instances the challenges you had previously identified are changing. You are hearing from more people, ideas are flowing, and even though the solution to the problem probably isn't perfect right away, things are noticeably better along a few key dimensions. You will have been observing, listening, and asking for feedback, and all signs are pointing to progress. Now you can bring what's working in your world and offer it to your peers. Perhaps when you attend the weekly meeting that someone else runs, and a need you're addressing is raised, you see an opportunity to explain to others what you and your team have done to identify and address it so far. And because you did the work to deeply understand the nature of the challenge, and were specific and clear about the new behaviors, you're able to share with others at a level of clarity that makes it easier for them to understand, appreciate, and adopt. Your precision will stand in stark contrast to some of your counterparts who are asked how they deliver great experiences or maximize productivity and respond with generalities like, "We make sure everyone is heard," or "We make sure people feel safe." As laudable as those are, they are difficult to understand, and so they're difficult to replicate and sustain.

Community as a stage in the cycle helps a small, isolated change spread and take root in other parts of the organization. Over time, some of what you develop and deploy may be so broadly applicable that it spreads simply because it's useful and appropriate, or because it catches the attention of senior leaders who identify your practice as one that may positively benefit other teams. As you check in regularly with your peers to see how they're faring and how you can help each other, be sure to share the wins and challenges, and to learn from each other.

If all of this has you thinking that this sounds like a lot of work, I certainly won't try to dissuade you of that notion. But with some helpful tips on building community, we can clarify the process and make it fulfilling to see an idea spread.

CHAPTER 8

Community Practice

Identify your crucial stakeholders, shift your perspective, and craft the story.

Building community is all about going from a tight group of your initial collaborators and partners, to preparing the insights and behaviors you've discovered for a broader audience. This, like everything we've discussed, takes intention, because as much as those earlier in the process were included, asked for their perspective, and brought along the journey, you're now bringing something a bit more complete to a set of stakeholders who may not see how they are affected by the problem or why they should be interested in the solution.

This stage is where you have to embrace your inner storyteller, salesperson, and marketer. For some leaders that can feel counterintuitive. A common perception is that if this change is better, and more than a few of us can see how this would benefit a collection of us, why should I have to put any effort into packaging it for others to get on board?

While that's a common reaction, it's also a bit misguided, and one that any good leader needs to recognize and discard. Just because something is important to you, doesn't mean it's important to others. Just because your initial partners participated in identifying the problem and crafting behaviors to address it, doesn't mean that this will rise to the level of importance for others. And even if it is important enough, how and when the message is delivered is pivotal to building community and expanding the reach of the work you're doing. Perhaps in an ideal world the message would matter regardless of the delivery or the messenger, but we're humans, and we need to understand how those humans work in order to achieve these goals for the company and for all those who stand to benefit.

The best awareness building and most delicately crafted behaviors don't mean as much if they can't spread beyond the confines of the original architects. It's like having the *Mona Lisa* in your basement. It may be nice for you and your immediate circle, but sharing it more broadly benefits a much larger audience.

Going from an internal change among that core group to a broader team or company-wide change of behaviors requires finesse. Now you must change your approach and your mindset to one that is singularly focused on social relationships. You exercised this muscle a bit in the Awareness stage, as you paid attention to the right questions to ask in order to fully understand the issue at hand; however, in that case, you were focused on listening and paraphrasing, to be sure you understood the other person. Now you're focused on listening and communicating, to be sure the other people understand *you*.

Building community around the behaviors you've identified is as much a matter of solving problems as it is selling a new vision for the way work can get done. It's creating a compelling case for why the effort required to try something new is going to be beneficial, and is worth the trouble. Remember, you're fighting against the status quo. Even if things aren't perfect, what's currently happening is what's familiar. The culture you have in your organization is the one that has been optimized to get things done right now. Changing culture one behavior at a time requires overcoming the inertia of history – "That's how we do things" – and apathy – "I don't think we can realistically do things differently."

To do this, you have to identify the right people, get inside their heads to find out what matters to them – which may not be the same as what they say matters to them – and sell them on a story that makes sense to their needs. Community is all about gaining buy-in by helping others see the problem and solution in ways that make sense to them, so that they feel compelled to join you on this journey.

Done well, you aren't pushing or dragging people along, because in that instance you will inadvertently start policing their actions or assume the role of their external motivator. Instead, when you connect the new behaviors to things they already care about, they will feel pulled by the strength of the change to head in the new direction on their own.

With all of that in mind, the Key 3 of Community are: *Identify your crucial stakeholders, Shift your perspective,* and *Craft the story.*

Identify Your Crucial Stakeholders

Eroding Action: Companies have a long and storied history of identifying a new action, behavior, process, or methodology, and very quickly doing their best to roll it out across a particular division or the entire company. If something is good, the thinking goes, then the best thing they can do is get everyone doing that thing as quickly as possible. By casting a wide net, they try to recruit everyone at once. Yet, in many instances, the goal isn't truly to recruit people to get behind a change, but to mandate it. The underlying premise is that someone knows best, usually one of the senior leaders, and this behavior is going to benefit everyone, so we all need to adopt it as quickly as possible. These announcements can often take the form of company-wide notes, launches, or large-scale promotions.

What makes this an eroding action is that these efforts are an example of going broad and shallow, where what we want at this point are efforts that are more narrow and deep. Identifying the crucial stakeholders is far more productive for the kind of change at hand. There are times when bold steps and broad communication are necessary. When the company is struggling financially and barely able to make payroll, or when it's dealing with an unforeseen crisis, immediate decisions need to be made. In these situations, the leader must be willing to acknowledge that moment in time as something different than culture change, and be held accountable for the quality and effectiveness of those decisions. Culture change isn't something anyone, even the most senior leaders, can just mandate. You must identify your crucial stakeholders, and productively engage them, before taking your narrative too broad.

It's more valuable, in other words, for you to get a significant commitment from a few partners than to get a mix of dismissive nods and loose agreement from a whole host of stakeholders. Going too broad too fast with the behaviors you've identified is likely to leave you struggling to juggle the depth of the commitment you need with the breadth of trying to engage too many stakeholders.

Instead, I generally recommend starting with three to five people whom you believe hold the keys to taking direct action, or are crucial to successfully engaging others. This range can be flexible depending on the size of the group you're looking to influence, but in my experience, I've found three to five to be a valuable starting point, whether I was changing behaviors at a 200-person company, or a 160,000-person company.

Three to five is right because these are the people you're bringing into the "inner circle" and asking for their support and contribution. Trying to manage too many relationships gets unwieldy and prohibits you from investing the right amount of energy into understanding their motivations. Any fewer than three, and you'll likely have trouble gaining traction, because you're drawing too narrow a field around who you should consider crucial. Here are some questions I like to ask myself to help identify my three to five crucial stakeholders:

- Were they already part of the Awareness or Behaviors stage? (If so, they're already involved and included. No need to add them here. Keep them engaged, but they're already part of the community.)
- Can their support *significantly* help spread the behavior?
- Can I *realistically* get their support?
- Can their resistance *significantly* halt the behavior?
- Might they *realistically* and *significantly* resist?

The value of asking yourself these questions, and answering them honestly, is that you can identify the critical few and start to see results much more quickly than you might have otherwise.

As much as I've tried to stay away from the corporate speak, there is a warning that fits quite well here: Don't try to boil the ocean. The basic premise being that by trying to take on something so large, the amount of energy is unreasonable, and the impacts are miniscule. Instead, focus on boiling a pot of water, and getting others to boil their own pots of water. As you start to see patterns and successes, you can expand the community and invite others in. And if the behaviors are working as you've intended, you'll find others start asking to be invited in and participate, because the results are speaking for themselves, and your community is speaking for whatever else needs to be said.

Shift Your Perspective

Eroding Action: Adopting the perspective of someone else isn't easy. We're naturally wired to see the world through our own eyes, and our brains are adept at convincing us that what we see is both real and right.[1] It takes practice to combat the feeling of certainty and accuracy to appreciate that what we believe is unique to us, and even more practice to genuinely try to understand what others may feel and believe. Leaders set themselves up for failure when they ignore what matters to others, and focus exclusively on what matters to them. In doing so, they orient the work and its relevance around them, and put themselves at the center. *Here's what I found. Here's what I've figured out. Here's what I need you to do.* Avoid this eroding behavior by shifting your perspective to truly understand what matters to the crucial stakeholders in your community and meet them where they are.

Some of the greatest lessons I've ever had about life and leadership have been taught to me by my family, sometimes completely by accident.

One such instance was a time when my eldest son and I were watching television together. He was around seven years old, and we were watching a fictional TV show that followed a collection of high school football players as they navigated school, becoming adults, and of course, football. In one scene, the quarterback was on the field, and the camera panned around from his perspective to show all the cheering fans in their seats, each one primed and ready for him to make the big final play and win the game. I turned to my son and mindlessly said, "Wouldn't you love to be on the field for an experience like that?," to which he replied in the sweetest and most easy-going tone, "Nah, I'd rather be in the stands."

At that moment, I realized I was applying my perspective to his world, and that to truly understand and engage him, I was going to learn to appreciate him for who he was, not for who I may have initially wanted him to be. And as his dad, who expects him to do certain chores and take up certain responsibilities around the house, if I framed those needs through my own view of the world, I would forever be wasting my time and frustrating us both. The end goal, whether it was encouraging him to try his best on the soccer pitch, or simply to clean up his room, had to be communicated through a lens of what was important to him. The failure to shift my perspective, and therefore to presume that the best path forward is simply to try harder to convince him that I'm right, he's wrong, and he's just not seeing things correctly, was a surefire way to see him become entrenched in his position, or go along simply to avoid a confrontation. But any behavior changes were likely to be short-lived.

While our co-workers are not our family, and certainly not our children, this lesson of shifting perspective served me well. Before you approach your crucial stakeholders you need to get into their world and understand what matters *to them*. The problem might simply not be on their radar like it has been for you. You've been immersed in this problem and solution for quite some time, learning about it, asking others about it, researching it, and establishing new behaviors to combat the issue. For your crucial stakeholders, this conversation may be new. So, you have to pause and reflect. Think about what they care about, and what they're trying to accomplish. Think about how this new set of behaviors helps them achieve something by connecting the efforts at hand to an issue they already acknowledge or one you can easily help them see as relevant. Research on negotiation over the decades has shown that what we say we value – our *positions* – don't always reflect what truly matters to us – our *interests*.[2] By digging below the surface to understand your crucial stakeholders' interests, you can more appropriately frame your solution in a way that matters to each of them, and also avoid the trap of thinking you have mutual agreement even though you're really talking past one another. This is a situation we want to avoid at all costs.

One helpful practice is to take the time to write down the names of your three to five crucial stakeholders, and for each stakeholder, write down why you believe they would say the problem you've identified matters.

This isn't what you would tell them to convince them, but rather what you expect you would hear if you asked them directly. If you're struggling with this, ask a trusted peer, perhaps one who was part of the Awareness stage. What goals does this stakeholder have that removing this problem would help solve?

In the next column, capture what about this change would likely be unappealing to them. If they were being honest, how would they say this might make their life more difficult? Are you seeing overlap among your stakeholders? If so, you may have identified points of leverage, or places of weakness in your strategy.

It should start to become clear in this exercise how to overcome certain objections, or how you might frame requests so that the person responds with an open mind. You also may see some opportunities to bring together crucial stakeholders, if their interests and concerns are aligned.

By taking the time to pause and reflect, your goal is to stop yourself from plowing ahead and erroneously assuming others have the same goals or concerns you do. And the more you do this kind of exercise, the better you get at understanding others. You'll figure out where you were accurate and where you were off.

Craft the Story

Eroding Action: A subtle and damaging behavior is operating with a presumption that the leader is "above" things like storytelling, and that if someone else needs a message delivered in a way they perceive as compelling and intentional, then that person is somehow not a serious person. Many companies are led by people who have long believed in the idea of completely rational people, or *Homo economicus*. These leaders look down on carefully framed narratives, choosing instead to believe that adults, especially those in serious businesses, should function dispassionately and evaluate each situation with an eye toward return on investment and overall utility. This isn't how most people work. To be clear, it's not even how markets work. Look back over history, and you'll see irrational, emotional decision-making everywhere you look, even in the most economically driven environments, like stock markets, real estate markets, and auctions.

Leaders who ignore the humanity of their peers and partners are likely to anchor their thinking on arguments that miss important aspects of what helps us share ideas, motivate actions, and sustain change. Stories help people put the change in context and visualize the future. Stories are crucial in the quest for progress.

On a daily and weekly basis, each of us is called on to sell. While we may not be trading a product for a currency, we may still find ourselves pitching our boss on a new project, lobbying for a promotion or raise for one of our employees, or convincing the group to select one vendor over another. In each of these situations, we're using our influence and expertise to get people to make a choice that we either don't have the authority to make alone, or that we want people to voluntarily get onboard with.

Culture change is a similar scenario. Culture change, like the other examples, won't get far with just facts alone. You must connect identifying your crucial stakeholders with shifting your perspective, and bring those together in a story that compellingly demonstrates how things will be better after this change.

Much of my early career was in retail. In some roles, I supported customers with their clothes purchases; in others I supported them with their electronics purchases.

Even when people came in to buy and had already decided they were planning to leave with something, I made sure to approach the sale with an important distinction in mind: turning features into benefits. The fabric of a shirt (feature) doesn't really matter, but you might be interested to know that it breathes and will allow you to be out with your significant other on a warm day without getting sweaty (benefit). Likewise, the hard drive space of a phone (feature) won't impress many people, but you might like to know that it can hold more photos of your children, dog, vacation, or whatever is most important to you (benefit).

So it is in business. At work, you might be getting ready to share your strategy with a person who often feels overwhelmed, and you would do well not just to tell them about the problems the new behaviors solve (features) but also how much new free time they'll have (benefits). For someone else, the benefits might speak to their preference for order and efficiency; for another, their opportunity to make a difference for customers or to improve the experience for job candidates.

While sales and marketing can have negative connotations for some, remember that each of the stories you present to your colleagues – each version, tweaked slightly to resonate with your audience of one – is true. Each of us comes to work with a different perspective and collection of needs and interests and gets something different out of the work we do. A major part of your job as a leader, and especially during this period of change, is to identify what motivates the people around you, and meet them where they are. An added benefit: People will tend to appreciate you for having taken the time to see things from their point of view.

Along the path, you may notice that your crucial stake-holders aren't consistent about the new behaviors, or perhaps they're doing them incorrectly. Assuming that you've clearly identified the behaviors and communicated them well, before you take any action it's worth considering the distinction we raised before. Are you and this person part of the same commune, or are you rather part of the same neighborhood? Remember that the commune has a direct impact on your ability to succeed. Their failure makes it difficult or impossible for you. As part of a neighborhood, you're partially isolated, and what another person does in their space may not impact you directly, at least not right away.

This distinction is important as you determine your next steps.

If you and the person are part of the same commune, it's important to address the inconsistency head-on. As you continue to build healthy relationships, you must trust they will respond productively when you raise what you're seeing. And yet, as we noted before, curiosity is a powerful skill. Getting at *why* they are doing what they are doing tends to be far more effective than trying to police their actions. Curiosity builds awareness; policing simply encourages them to hide things from you. Chances are, if you are curious and timely with raising your questions, they will be more likely to thank you than be resentful for recognizing their challenges with the behaviors. I've even had success prefacing such questions with the fact that I'd want the other person to tell me if I was doing something contrary to an agreement we'd made. Highlighting the reciprocity involved in your relationship can remind them that you're on a team, and you're in this together.

On the other hand, if they are part of your neighborhood, tread more lightly. It's important in a healthy and performance-oriented culture that we all hold each other accountable, but still better to lead with seeking to understand. You may choose to observe for a bit longer and see if the stakeholder is just working through the change. Since their actions don't directly impact your standing or well-being, best to let the situation play out in their own space before deciding if it's truly worth intervening for the sake of the group.

Over time, as you build a stronger and healthier community, you should notice a "flywheel effect," as Jim Collins describes in his book *Good to Great*.[3] Collins observed that some organizations, through the consistency of their actions, almost seem to be pushing over and over on a metaphorical flywheel. As their actions accumulate, the wheel begins to generate momentum, and eventually it takes less effort to keep the flywheel moving. People who become accustomed to changes, knowing you're leading them somewhere productive and have their interests in mind, won't take as long to get on board. You'll know the flywheel is humming just as it should.

CHAPTER 9

Systems Cement the Change

How to make your culture run (almost) on autopilot.

Before we explore the final step in the ABCS, let's pause for a brief recap.

At this point we've identified the right problem to solve, and gotten clear on exactly what the problem is. That's Awareness. We've also clearly defined and described the actions that we believe will help solve the problem at hand. That's Behaviors. We've then rallied and educated a group to help spread the word, and spread the behaviors, to be sure that the work doesn't rest solely with a few people who might struggle to keep things moving forward on their own. In that sense, we've democratized the problem and the behaviors by bringing others along. That's Community.

Now we're looking to drive these changes deeper into the fabric of the company, through intentionally and confidently crafting systems that make it clearer and easier to perform the behaviors over and over again.

The first three elements of the ABCS model enable us to get things right some of the time. Systems enable us to get things right most of the time. The difference between a team that harnesses creativity some of the time, and a team that has systems that support repeatable behaviors that harness creativity most of the time, is profound. Think of the most creative companies you know. I'm willing to bet that each of them has gone beyond solving the challenge right in front of them, to build systems that make it easier for employees to follow the right behaviors that drive and support creativity. Systems build consistency by reducing the effort required to perform the right behaviors.

Think of it this way: In many instances, a key difference between a bottom-tier professional sports team and a world-class championship team is consistency over time. Whether in basketball, soccer, hockey, or any other high-level event, the highest-performing teams can run the right plays, in the right formations, at just the right time, *almost every time*. They create surrounding systems to help those behaviors become fluid and easier, because it's crucial that everyone understands what's about to happen and what role each person plays. These teams build the right processes and practices to be able to deliver, especially when time is tight and tensions are high. The systems are what make the difference between the teams that tend to fall apart when the score is close or players get injured, and the teams that can adapt and adjust, based on the circumstances. Does your team collaborate when it's convenient, or are you a team that creates space to collaborate? Are you building a team that is inclusive when there's time, or are you building a team that creates the conditions to be inclusive and produce better outcomes?

Systems can generally be defined in two ways: fluid systems and fixed systems. Fluid systems are those that gently guide behavior. They are things like policies, procedures, principles, or protocols (although they don't always have to start with P!). These systems are ones that we've agreed to, communicated, and expect people to follow. Generally speaking, they are the ways work gets done, and they serve as the reinforcements for the behaviors you expect to see in the organization.

So when we say that we expect people to leave time at the end of a meeting for quiet reflection before opening it up to comments and closing thoughts, a fluid system might be defining who's keeping time, clarifying how much time, and articulating what happens after that time is complete.

A fixed system, however, is more like a mandate. Sometimes it's hard coded into a platform or piece of software. Sometimes it's a specific punitive threat, a known consequence for misaligned behavior. A fixed system is something that makes it incredibly difficult to do anything other than the behavior that has been defined. It's so embedded into a way of working that you would actually need to circumvent some process, and if you were caught, there would be repercussions so severe that overriding the system won't be worth the effort for most people.

For instance, let's imagine a hospital that implements both kinds of systems. This hospital has identified after careful analysis that it inadvertently disadvantages male nurses in the hiring process. For whatever reason, perhaps related to bias, qualified men are being hired at far lower rates than equally qualified women. The hospital decides that to reap the benefits of demographic diversity, and more closely match its patient composition, this needs to change. And so the hospital's talent leaders go through the ABCS process. Through awareness building they target the interview portion of the hiring process as a place for change. They determine that they will implement a few deliberate behaviors, which include deploying a standard set of questions in each interview, employing a three-person interview panel – where three members of the current staff interview each applicant, in order to share thoughts and notes – and as a final step, each member of the panel will score each applicant on a rubric that lays out the criteria by which the applicant should be evaluated. Underneath each of these headers are the specific behaviors that lay the foundation for what needs to happen.

Now envision that in order to embed these behaviors into the hospital, they first consider a fluid system, where there is agreement that every member of interviewing panels will use these criteria and resources to assess applicants. Then they consider a more fixed system, where before an interviewer can provide their recommendation about whether or not to move forward with a candidate, they must submit that completed rubric to the person in charge of the hiring process. Finally, we can envision an even more fixed system where the hospital invests in applicant-tracking technology that will not allow an applicant to move through the process until the interview panel uploads their scores and feedback, thereby removing the ability to circumvent the system.

The hospital will need to decide which system is most appropriate to suit their needs. Which system will simultaneously reinforce the desired behaviors without creating any negative unintended consequences, such as a lack of trust or feelings of micromanagement?

While it will always be possible to get around a system, we see that as we move from fluid to fixed, we increase the effort required to go around the desired behavior. If a hiring manager wanted to simply ask their own questions and "go with their gut," they would need to ignore the provided questions, turn the other panel members into co-conspirators, and fabricate answers to the rubric, all to avoid following the path that has been laid out. In this case, it's easier to perform the desired behaviors than it is to work against them.

When it's harder to avoid the right behaviors, you have a stubbornly fixed system. And *stubborn* is the right word, because the more fixed a system is, the more challenging it will be to cheat. These fixed systems are often more challenging to implement, and they are more difficult to undo. They also run the risk of signaling to employees that a more fluid system won't do, because people can't be trusted to follow it. You might not know intuitively at the start which kind of system will work best, because you've never done this before, so I often advise leaders to start with a fluid system. They are easier to implement and easier to undo. This is also part of why the ABCS are a cycle, because you want to iterate, learn, and take in feedback before you entrench a fixed system. It's important to be sure you know what you're committing to before you make it too difficult to do otherwise.

Fluid systems are not the same as weak systems, and fixed systems are not the same as strong systems. A system can be fluid and flexible, yet still be quite strong, like bamboo. A fixed system can be staunch and immovable, like a redwood tree. Neither is inherently better or worse, but the right system depends on where you are in your journey, and what level of confidence you have that you've nailed the right behaviors for the time being.

Far too often, fixed systems are used in place of spending the time earlier in the process. At times, instead of clarifying the problem, identifying the behaviors, or building community, it can be easy to just lay down a path and force people to travel it. But *easy* does not mean *sustainable*, nor does it mean *effective*. If the hospital had gone straight for the most rigid and high-tech fixed system, it might have accomplished its goal, but caused collateral damage to other parts of the culture. That's ultimately a bad system. Systems are meant to support the right behaviors and get out of the way. They aren't meant to be overkill by supporting the right behaviors at all costs.

Systems are important because they provide routines for the way behaviors get done. That takes effort and cognitive load off of the people involved, since they no longer need to worry about the logistics each time. We each have a limited amount of resources to dedicate to decisions and activities during any given day, and making certain behaviors easier and repeatable means that we free up those resources to focus on the things that matter.[1] Many people have heard of Silicon Valley executives who wear the same clothes routinely, in an effort to reduce what's known as "decision fatigue."[2] This is similar, except instead of you donning the same black t-shirt each day, your culture is donning the same process to support the behaviors you've identified.

Another reason systems matter is that they make the process to support the right behaviors generalizable. Nobody needs to be the hero. By removing the supporting system from an individual to a process, that system goes on regardless of changes to the team, as people join, leave, get busy, go on vacation, or feel overworked. The system is always in the background, lifting up the right behaviors.

In some cases, a person may be the one who is the main actor or resource in the system, but a person cannot be the system. If supporting the desired behavior all rests with one person, then the system is inherently fragile. Systems are the supporting mechanics that make the behaviors easier, and generalizing it to the function, not the person, keeps the system working well.

Within every team, it should be clear that if the person who ordinarily carries out the system is absent or can't perform their duties, someone else could easily fill in for them. They may not manage the system as well as the regular person, but ideally there are instructions laid out in process documents or a shared repository for how the system can be run for anyone who may be new to that system. For example, if a team has identified that in many instances their team meetings seem productive, but after the meeting they regularly struggle to recall what actions were committed to, who is accountable for what, and what comes next, a helpful behavior for creating clarity might be emailing meeting notes to the group.

A poor system would be: "Terry emails the notes to everyone." What if Terry leaves, or isn't at one of the meetings? What form do the notes take? How soon after the meeting should the notes be sent out? A better system is more specific in the actions and more generalizable in execution: "Within two hours after the meeting, the team's designated notetaker adds notes to this shared document, which we've previously organized by agenda topics."

It's worth noting that the connection between behaviors and systems, especially fluid systems, can feel messy at times. This is because almost everything we do at work is a behavior. It's an action being taken, and we take lots of actions every day. Even awareness building technically involves "actions," such as reading, listening, interviewing, and taking notes. What differentiates the behaviors from the systems is a question of understanding what truly matters. What are we trying to solve? That's Awareness. How are we going to solve that? Those are the Behaviors. What support do we need to put in place to reinforce the behaviors? Those are the Systems. Teams that regularly confuse systems with behaviors are likely to spend time and energy focused on the details and the mechanics, while missing the bigger picture. Systems are like backup dancers: They are valuable and useful for supporting the show, but they aren't the star performer. Just a few behaviors will get you where you want to go, and there will be lots of ways to build a system that supports those behaviors.

You may wonder how you will know when the time is right to increase the rigidity of your system. If you have a fluid system, and things are going pretty well, that may be the right time to transition to a fixed system. The two biggest questions to answer, though, are how confident you are that you have the right behaviors, and how confident you are that you won't want to change things for a while.

The answer to those queries will help you determine how fluid or fixed your system should be. If your behaviors seem to be humming along, well-supported, you might consider if there are other reasons to change the system, which might potentially upend things. Likewise, if you anticipate any big shake-ups on your team in the coming months, such as personnel changes or shifts in strategy, that may influence your decision. If things seem to be going smoothly, with no major changes in the foreseeable future, it may be best to let your fluid system keep humming along.

But let's say your answers to those questions are different. Maybe your team is on the brink of a major change, one that gives you reasons to think the fluid system you've relied on for so long might finally need to evolve into a more fixed system.

For example, imagine you find that there are pay gaps in your organization that ought to be closed. Perhaps through your awareness building, you determine that the best path forward is to standardize elements of the pay structure and remove some of the subjectivity around overall compensation. You bring people along, explain the rationale, and build energy around making more fair and objective compensation decisions. In this case, you might decide that when any pay offer is outside of the approved parameters it requires approval. That approval could be through technology, or it could be through an organizational escalation. It may be that a fixed system is appropriate in this case, because the repercussions for getting compensation decisions wrong have far-reaching impacts that you don't feel comfortable assuming. In this case a fixed system may be the right path forward. But you must still remember that locking yourself into a process doesn't excuse you from challenging and interrogating that process. It may be that the new compensation approvals or new compensation technology don't actually solve the pay disparities, and you may need to continue to investigate where the root of the problem lies. Your hypothesis about the right behaviors to embed may turn out to be fully, or partially, incorrect. That's okay, and it's to be expected. Just don't let a fixed system force you into making a commitment to a flawed set of behaviors. The essence of all of this work is to find the right problems to solve, find the right behaviors that lead to solutions, build the best culture you can, and provide value to your stakeholders. No one gets there on the first try, and no one stays there without consistent effort and humility.

While it's not a perfect metaphor, I like to think of fluid systems similar to dating, and fixed systems more like being married. Simply because a couple isn't married doesn't mean they're not serious, and getting married too soon can be disastrous if you haven't thought about the implications deeply enough. In addition, while a fixed system can be undone, it will likely entail a sizable degree of costs and disruption, much like the costs and disruption involved with ending a marriage. Fluid systems don't come with the same permanence; ending them may be challenging, but the collateral damage is usually less severe.

Fluid systems can provide a chance to learn and experiment, providing an element of structure and support without the costs associated with reversing a decision. Fixed systems provide rigor and discipline, and can be difficult to unwind if you find that you've made a mistake or the environment has changed so much that the system must also change. Across your organization you'll have a multitude of systems, and in each instance you need to build the systems that work for you, and let the needs of the team guide you toward formalizing those systems – spending money and time on bespoke solutions, higher technology, and so on.

To see systems in action, let's meet Marta. Marta is the chief people officer at her company. Through feedback, observation, and exit interviews from departing employees, Marta learns that many in her company are struggling with providing feedback about what they believe to be the start of toxic behaviors by senior leaders in the organization. Marta is honestly shocked, because she's never experienced these kinds of issues, and the past few weeks have been the first time she's heard about it. The exit interviews are especially enlightening, because people feel more comfortable saying what they've experienced, but Marta knows that even this feedback may be filtered because people don't want to burn bridges on their way out. With this new information, Marta goes on a mission of awareness building, setting up coffee chats with small groups of employees, asking open-ended questions, talking to her network of other Human Resources professionals to see what they've experienced and done, and reading what she can find about toxic behaviors and how to combat them.

After a brief period of education, Marta feels prepared to introduce some new behaviors to the organization. During her Awareness phase, Marta learned the top behavior routinely highlighted as toxic was tenured employees and managers discounting the contributions of newer employees. Specifically, senior people were taking credit for junior people's work, either accidentally or not, by always being the ones to present ideas to clients and executives, and not highlighting the contributions of the entire team. That lack of credit is making more junior people feel unappreciated.

When Marta shares this feedback at a meeting of her peers, they're surprised as well. None of them wants to make people feel overlooked, but they're also concerned about creating a culture where everyone gets a pat on the back for everything they do. In partnership with a small cross-functional team, Marta identifies a handful of behaviors that a couple of teams in the company will pilot. These behaviors include adding the names of all participating team members to the last slide of the presentation deck, almost like the credits in a movie, and selectively rotating which members of the team get to present ideas or be in key meetings where the final product is being delivered.

Along the way, while collecting what's working and what's not, Marta and the pilot groups are building systems – clearly defining roles and responsibilities to support the behaviors that they can now see and hear. Marta has added a fluid system where there is a role designated on the project team to build the aforementioned slide. Marta and some teams are testing another system that tracks who presents in idea pitches and key meetings, so that they can put data around this issue. The hypothesis is that adding data will help this behavior shift for their more metrics-oriented employees. At some point Marta thinks she might invest in creating an internal site where, before any project can be closed, the team leader must add every member who worked on the project, so that everyone across the company can see who contributed to the success of each body of work. But for now, that's just an idea. The fluid systems seem to be working, and Marta is getting feedback that people increasingly feel recognized and appreciated, and that the behaviors and accompanying systems aren't burdensome or time intensive.

What did Marta do well? She listened, acted, and is seeing the benefits in increased engagement, greater productivity, and lower attrition. Now Marta is staying attuned to any unintended consequences, while simultaneously turning her attention to another cultural element that she wants to refine. And given how Marta is getting comfortable with the ABCS cycle, and bringing others along with her, the next challenge doesn't seem quite so daunting.

To be like Marta, we need to make our systems powerful yet simple. Complicated systems overwhelm employees, and can unintentionally become the focal point, where our goal is to make the behaviors the focal point. Over time, good systems fade into the background. They move closer into the land of habits, where actions are performed instinctually and without as much intentional thought as behaviors. We may consciously know the value of sharing a document, taking notes, or sending out post-meeting insights, but we don't devote as much brain power to those actions as we do the behaviors they support. They are powerful, because they allow the key behaviors to flourish within a team, but they are also simple, requiring a small amount of effort to sustain that doesn't leave any one person feeling overwhelmed.

Attentive leaders will still keep their eyes and ears open for when systems are breaking down, which shouldn't be too difficult because inefficiencies show themselves as friction when the behaviors are clearly articulated and well understood. If the system breaks down, the behavior breaks down, too. In this friction, poor systems make themselves known, which means you can easily address them by changing the system to reduce friction, or by swapping a new system in for the existing one.

Getting at the difference between a fluid system and a fixed one, or removing the friction from a system, are all part of making the systems stick. Our practice chapter cements these ideas and gives you the tools to bring together getting systems right.

CHAPTER 10

Systems Practice

Anticipate and evaluate, map the flow, and keep systems supportive.

Systems can be sneaky. They are deceptively important for solving a problem once and for all, and at the same time notoriously difficult to get right. But they're worth it, because when you identify and implement the right systems to support the desired behaviors, everyone is likely to feel the difference. Work gets more fluid, because the systems are nudging us in the direction that supports the optimal behaviors. Interactions are smoother because there's less ambiguity around what matters to keep the behaviors central and alive. Projects seem to come together with fewer setbacks, because the effort to future-proof the project, before it's even begun, creates greater seamlessness.

This Systems practice chapter is all about how to differentiate between a helpful system and an unhelpful one, along with how to communicate the systems you're building to your new community of stakeholders and colleagues.

Before you implement any systems, however, it's helpful to run a bit of a thought experiment, during which you once again pause and think about how what you're building is going to affect others. As we've discussed, both fluid and fixed systems have a material impact on how others are able to get their work done, whether the desired behavior is made easier or more challenging, and to what degree you influence or bind people to certain actions. Before you deploy a system that you've only marginally considered, you need to flex that perspective-taking muscle you built in the Community stage and capture some notes on how you anticipate a given system working. Run through scenarios in your head to more fully appreciate the benefits, drawbacks, and overall implications of your proposed system.

Once you've decided on the right systems, you'll need to socialize them with the people who will be using them. You've perhaps been alone doing this portion of the work related to building a system, so it's imperative to take a step back and engage others around the broader context for the change and what you expect of them. As with our other steps, there is a back and forth of work you do alone or in a small group, and work you do collectively, by bringing the system to the broader population.

Lastly, you'll need to ensure the systems stay systems. There's a tendency for systems to start to be perceived more like the critical behaviors, rather than *supporting* the critical behaviors. When systems are confused for behaviors, the effect on the community can be that teams start simply going through the motions of completing a checklist, where in reality behaviors should solve a real problem.

Together, these priorities create a Key 3 of: *Anticipate and evaluate, Map the flow,* and *Keep systems supportive.*

Anticipate and Evaluate

Eroding Action: As a leader confronted with such a wide variety of problems, issues, and setbacks on any given day, optimism is a useful outlook. Optimism becomes a liability, however, when we fail to acknowledge and appreciate the things that might go wrong. With all of the energy and momentum from identifying the problem, building behaviors, and rallying the community, it's easy to get overwhelmed by that momentum and forget that the future is unknown, and there are lots of ways our plans may not come together exactly how we anticipate. We can't just hope it works out. We must have a healthy degree of skepticism that things might break or fail and plan for those scenarios. Failure to do that, and instead assuming that it will all resolve itself, can leave gaps unidentified, partners frustrated, and plans unexecuted. While subtle, unrealistic optimism in the form of ignoring possible roadblocks can wear away at productive culture change.

The work you did in the Awareness phase helped you home in on a clearly identified problem. Then you moved to defining a clear solution in the form of specific behaviors. And yet, even the best strategists are susceptible to getting things wrong. We can never know how the underlying conditions and assumptions that led to our decisions will shift under our feet as the environment changes. What you knew for sure was a necessary change might need further tweaking.

That's why it's important to do scenario planning at the beginning of the Systems stage. You need to sit by yourself or with your team and come up with several scenarios for how a given system might play out. Ask yourself a handful of seemingly simple questions, such as:

- If we move ahead with this plan, what's likely to happen?
- How will people respond?
- What other, perhaps competing, incentives do we have in place that might supersede this system?

That last question may be the most important.

Too often, I've seen leadership teams come up with policies that seem well-intentioned but in reality are divorced from how the organization is set up to operate, because the new behaviors and systems come into direct conflict with other, higher priorities. What happens is the higher-order priority wins out, and the system is relegated to a memory, or a joke.

For instance, envision a company that recognizes employees are regularly feeling burned out. Sick time is up, morale is down, people aren't proactively taking time away, and all of this is affecting productivity, engagement, and retention. People are working too hard for too long, and then simply walking away to join a competitor. Or, as my mother always told me, "If you don't treat people well, they'll quit and leave, or they'll quit and stay." So perhaps instead of people leaving once they're burned out, they spend far more energy trying to stay under the radar, avoid getting additional work, and preserve their well-being by disconnecting.

Let's say the leaders of these teams recognize this problem of burnout and decide that the right thing to do is to institute a minimum amount of time away that each employee needs to take. They may have heard about other companies that realized people needed a bit more guidance around productively disconnecting from work, and have similarly deployed a mandate (a fixed system) where employees need to take off at least three weeks a year.

But what happens if the expectations around performance and output don't align with this new mandate? What if employees start to feel that they're at risk of losing their jobs or missing out on a promotion because they can't realistically step away and still meet their targets? What if the people who regularly get recognized and rewarded are the ones who work during their "vacation" or cut short their time away to come back and perform heroics for the company?

In this case, what the company purports to care about – time away to recharge in order to come back to work ready to perform at a high level – is regularly being undercut by the actual, hidden priorities.

I'd often see this same thing in companies with whom I was consulting, as they'd say that inclusive behaviors were a top priority, and then continue to promote leaders who brought in significant business but were widely known to be incredibly challenging to work with. You can probably guess which behaviors employees modeled: the ones the company said mattered (inclusion, collaboration) or the ones the company actually rewarded (selfishness). Employees are influenced less by the culture being described and more by the culture being reinforced and rewarded. A business school classmate once said, "You can't talk your way out of something you acted your way into." The misalignment between what's said and what's valued can significantly undermine change efforts.

Sometimes the actions a company takes diverge so severely from the goal it's trying to achieve, or the problem it's trying to solve, that the "solution" actually makes things worse. These mismatched priorities are what economists call "perverse incentives."[1] Because perverse incentives can do so much damage to the culture that's being built, it's worth looking at an example.

Imagine an organization where the problem they identify is a lack of recognition. Through Awareness, Behaviors, and Community, they believe that the path forward is to create a recognition platform where employees can recognize each other with small awards or cash prizes, and to incentivize employees to participate, each recognition of someone else gets the nominator entered into a drawing for a cash bonus. At the end of the quarter, a drawing will take place, and a random nominator will get this bonus. The more you recognize others, the greater your chances of winning the cash bonus. Sounds great, but things can quickly go awry.

Within a short time, people may realize they can increase their chances of a bonus by "recognizing" others for traits that they don't actually notice or believe in, just to get as many entries into the raffle as possible. Now if you're the person being recognized by your co-workers you might not feel the same if you thought they were trying to game the system. And it might soon become apparent that recognition has gone way up in quantity, but actual feelings of recognition have potentially gone way down.

By taking an altruistic behavior – showing recognition – and tying it to a monetary reward, the organization has created perverse incentives, and the system became corrupted.

A relatively simple exercise that can expose some gaps in your planning, and hopefully avoid creating perverse incentives, is to jot down how the system will perform best-case, most-likely, and worst-case. While the exercise won't catch everything, it will catch far more than simply rushing ahead. In addition, given the inherent ambiguity in a new system, you'll want to wait to evaluate what you put in place until at least the 30-day mark. Thirty days gives the system enough time to sink into the daily work, and for people to adjust to the new process.

Within those 30 days you'll likely hear from people who love it and people who hate it, and both of those reactions may be simply because it's new. It's not until you're through the initial phase of deployment that you can really understand how people are affected by the new systems. You'll need to look and listen for both quantitative and qualitative feedback: Are people performing the behavior more times per week (quantitative)? Are they saying good things to one another about the new system (qualitative)? There will be many signals as to whether to keep the system in place, make slight tweaks, or go back to the start.

Map the Flow

Eroding Action: Speed in business is key. We tend to make decisions quickly, take actions quickly, and make changes quickly. But in the rush of finalizing a big change, or even a small one, leaders can't forget that they rely on other people's help to be successful. Leaders can initiate a change, but they can't unilaterally make a change stick. Thinking they can do it all themselves, or failing to give people the broader context for the change, will lead to frustration and lack of results. All of the work may wind up being fruitless. Seeing how the new system works in your mind's eye is useful, but capturing how this new system fits into existing processes, in a way that others can see and understand, is vital. Assuming that your understanding will translate into an accurate and complete understanding for others is an eroding action, and will eat away at the efficiency of your efforts.

Mapping the flow is a precursor to cementing the change, where, similar to the Community stage, you once again appreciate that you cannot do this work alone. What's different at this stage is that you're informing others more than you are soliciting their input. You've already done that work, getting broad buy-in to help you with addressing the problem and deploying the behavior as a solution. Now it's time to let people know what's about to happen.

If we picture the culture change as going on a road trip, you've already recruited people to come with you – your passengers are along for the ride. Now you need to tell them what vehicle you're taking, who's responsible for driving which legs of the trip, how many stops you'll make, where you'll stop, and so on. Mapping the flow is all about the logistics of the implementation, so people know why they're asked to make a change and what's expected of them. Barring this, you're simply telling people, "Get in the car and let's go."

As far as the tactical process of mapping the flow, I've seen this done in a variety of ways, and your company practices may guide you toward which is most acceptable and digestible. Some people use presentation decks, while others prefer to use mind-mapping programs that can serve as a kind of digital whiteboard. Still others prefer hand-drawn roadmaps. How you map the flow for your team and organization will depend on the scale of the culture-change initiative and the number of people involved.

What's also important, alongside the graphic representation of this change and how it fits into the existing process, is how you communicate. This includes things like your framing, positioning, and tone. You likely know more about this problem than your target audience does, because you've spent time researching and investigating it. Just as they know more about their area of expertise, you've become a subject matter expert in this issue. But a good subject matter expert doesn't lead with superiority; they use their expertise to take things that may seem unapproachable or complex, and make them easier and less cumbersome. Be sure to frame your messaging in a way that signals this desire to support and empower others, and that you are lightly turning people's shoulders to support them to see what you see, rather than trying to pry their eyes open against their will.

The Irish playwright George Bernard Shaw is reported to have said, "The single biggest problem in communication is the illusion that it has taken place."[2] You can help ensure communication happens by working hard to put in the work and map out the flow, verbally and visually. The following offers a handful of alternatives to common missteps in mapping the flow.

Instead of:
- Telling people what you have found
- Giving an impression that everything is already figured out
- Overselling the problem
- Assuming the problem and solution are self-evident
- Anchoring on either the narrative or the visual

Try:
- Telling people what others have shared
- Inviting people to be part of the deployment and giving feedback

- ◆ Conveying why this matters, in real language
- ◆ Speak and map the problem
- ◆ Use the narrative and the visual to capture different listeners

It's vital that people come away from this communication feeling like the new systems address a genuine pain point – and even if one employee hasn't yet felt that pain personally, they can see from how you've mapped the flow that it's for the good of the group that they come along.

Keep Systems Supportive

Eroding Action: Confusion halts progress. It doesn't always slam on the brakes or grind things to a complete stop, but it does introduce unproductive friction. This kind of friction slows momentum and increases the effort needed to move things ahead. When it comes to keeping systems supportive, leaders sometimes fail to differentiate the behavior from the system, and to keep that clear in the actions of the team. Leaders who become overly invested in the mechanics of the system, as opposed to anchoring on the identified behavior as the crucial point of leverage, can confuse employees as to what matters. That confusion erodes trust in the process and belief in the competence of the leader. But rarely does that happen immediately; it's the ongoing chipping away that makes confusion about behaviors and systems something to avoid.

Remember that systems are the back-up dancers, and the behaviors are the star of the show. The behavior is the action people take so that they avoid the problem that was identified in the Awareness phase. Its purpose is to create more helpful situations that tilt the company in the right direction, action by action, step by step. The system, however, is the surrounding and supporting set of actions that make the behavior easier to perform, by removing obstacles and smoothing the path. The system doesn't solve the problem.

In the minimum vacation mandate example from earlier, the systems may make it easier to request vacation, or more difficult to accumulate vacation, or automate an out-of-office message so that people don't feel compelled to think of one themselves. But those are all in support of the behavior around employees taking a specific range of vacation days in a year.

While both the articulation of the problem and the right set of behaviors will be slightly unique to most teams and experiences, here are a few examples to highlight the differences:

Problem: Poor ongoing communication about goals and objectives

Behavior: Weekly check-in

Systems: Immovable check-ins, check-in template, monthly reporting on compliance

Problem: Missed deadlines

Behavior: Escalation when project is in danger

Systems: On-time percent tied to bonuses, automated emails to executive sponsors when deadlines are missed

Problem: Poor clarity about project roles

Behavior: All projects start with structured kick-off

Systems: Project management tools, internal site communicating project roles, training

Problem: Lack of internal career progression

Behavior: Internal candidates interviewed first

Systems: Job posting overhaul, pre-filled resumes for current employees, promotion/movement targets

As organizations grow, and the initial underlying challenge is addressed through behaviors and systems, companies and teams inevitably make changes. I envision new behaviors like a tree sapling: fragile and growing. Systems are like the stakes one might tether to the sapling, to help it grow straight and tall, and guide it through the early periods where it may be too weak to stand on its own. The stakes protect it from strong winds that would otherwise knock the sapling down, the same way that systems protect new behaviors that might fall victim to other priorities. Yet at some point the stakes constrain the growth of the tree, and either need to be replaced or removed, because they are no longer necessary. Such is the case with systems. Certain systems may eventually become obsolete, at times because the behaviors are strong enough to stand on their own as they are fully integrated into the culture or because things have changed enough that the systems no longer supply the right level of support. As the saying goes, what got you here won't get you there.

As the systems are no longer necessary, you can evaluate whether you need new and evolved systems, or if the behavior is strong enough and embedded enough to stand on its own. This is part of why fluid systems can still have a place in a long-term strategy. Fluid systems, as we explored, are easier to undo. They are easier to walk away from when the time is right. While fixed systems may be harder to undo, they too have a natural expiration date, when the policy, platform, or penalty is no longer serving to reinforce a necessary behavior. Staying attentive to when systems have run their course is challenging, because they can quickly become the status quo, and inertia and fear of change can make us hold onto systems that have out-lived their usefulness. The best way to check a system's usefulness is against the behavior. If the behavior needs rethinking, the system necessarily does, too. Observing through an impartial lens to determine when systems have run their course will help you keep supporting the right behaviors that fit with how your organization is evolving.

To illustrate the tension with a good system, we can look toward some retirement plans. Certain US companies have a retirement plan where you can contribute a certain portion of your income, the company will match a portion of what you save, and that money is invested according to your wishes.

Without getting too deep into the logistics, the under-lying intent is to save money for when the worker gets older, so that they can retire with funds they might not have if they hadn't saved. Research shows that employees whose savings rates are set by their employer, meaning that employees have to opt out of the plan instead of having to opt in, tend to save much more.[3] And many employees pick a set percent of their pay and rarely if ever adjust that amount. Each of these can be thought of as systems that reinforce the general behavior of saving. Hav-ing money automatically deducted from your paycheck means you don't have to think about it each time. Having a default rate set when you are hired reduces your need to make a decision. Putting your money into a particular fund means it can grow on your behalf.

All of these are arguably good things. But the system may no longer meet your needs if your situation changes. Saving for retirement may no longer be your main priority, or it may become even more of a priority. The fund you chose may be underperforming, and you'd do well to move your money. This highlights the tension of systems. They are valuable because they allow you to do something once and let that activity perpetuate. But that doesn't mean you can "set it and forget it." Low oversight shouldn't be confused with no oversight.

Systems are the final pieces of the ABCS and culture change puzzle. They bring the picture together so you can cement the culture you've been envisioning and working toward. As with the other three elements, when done well and with the right degree of intention, they tend to require more effort than you might expect.

At first, systems are noticeable because they are new policies and procedures that you didn't have before. They are novel and draw attention. They require effort and cognitive resources. But we lose sight of good systems eventually, because that's the point. Systems are meant to fade into the background and nudge with a guiding hand, either gently, as with fluid systems, or with a bit more sternness, in the case of fixed systems.

One of the traps we must actively avoid is thinking that because systems become subtle that they don't require much work on the front end to get them right, or ongoing work to keep them useful. There are a dizzying number of systems that can seem feasible or appropriate at first glance, yet often through added scrutiny you'll find that you're really talking about core behaviors, which we've seen must supersede the systems, or you're identifying the wrong systems that will incentivize the wrong behaviors.

People who architect and implement working systems are nothing less than artists. They require a keen understanding of a company's current incentives, how the culture operates, and what motivates people. They make the effort to go beyond simply looking, to really see what's happening at the company. They go beyond listening, to really understand what's happening around them. I invite you to see yourself as an artist, one who's sculpting a culture by adding or removing just the right elements so that there's a kind of elegance to the way work gets done – not by brute force or abuses of power, but by the right behaviors easily supported by the right systems.

CHAPTER 11

Putting It All Together

When effective culture just looks like high performance.

We've been on quite the journey together. We've worked through the high-level concepts and the lower-level logistics that embed effective activities as an essential component of great performance in organizations.

It's a good time to come back to the beginning, where we started our journey.

We began with the recognition that in far too many companies, and perhaps in yours, work isn't working. In an effort to understand and appreciate differences and similarities, we are now tripping up over terminology and points of view that often distract us from core aspects of work. We struggle to come together and harness our differences to deliver outstanding results, because we aren't clear about the behaviors and collaboration that allow us to do our best work. It's not just workplace distractions getting in the way, however. There are so many interests from outside the office begging to be addressed, through our inboxes, social media feeds, text messages, and TV broadcasts. Yet we must accept that even though we are thoughtful and concerned people, and creating some degree of separation can be challenging, it is imperative. We must ask what aspects of our lives are truly necessary to bring to work.

Too much of the conversation around workplace culture has said that if any part of us is held back, then we're not being true to ourselves. And yet the counter to that argument is that we are all slightly different versions of ourselves in different contexts. We adjust to our environment when we're out for a relaxed evening with close friends, or at a holiday dinner with our parents and family. We adjust for a night out at an art museum or an opera versus an evening at a comedy show or a concert. And yet we are still essentially ourselves. Choosing to bring our whole *work self* to work is a powerful choice, and it allows us to get the most out of ourselves and out of each other, while recognizing that except in very rare instances, work isn't meant to be all-consuming.

Each of us has a job because the organization where we work identified a set of goals that it believed were worth going after, to advance its position in the market, and decided someone ought to own a set of responsibilities that move the company toward those goals. Our workplaces are where we fulfill that duty. The desire to turn the workplace into a solution for the failures that we may perceive from other institutions is reasonable, yet misguided. Now we're far enough into our time together that you know this isn't an excuse to go back to a time where the majority had their say and everyone in the minority just needed to be happy to be allowed to have a job. None of what we've explored is an excuse to abuse people, reject humanity, create a toxic workplace, or otherwise disenfranchise employees. In fact, it's the opposite.

Work should be a harmonizing experience. We know that we perform better in workplaces that are safe – physically, emotionally, and psychologically. We know that teams with different backgrounds, and different demographics, outperform when it comes to challenging, nonroutine, creative tasks. We know that companies that treat their people well perform better, make more money, have lower retention costs, and are overall just more resilient. This is why in this book we've evaluated leadership and culture change through a lens that includes DEI. When we look through that lens including DEI, we recognize how work ought to function, and we see that it all boils down to performance.

The answer to finding balance at work is not to strip away all emotion, fun, and camaraderie. A blunt answer to a nuanced situation is almost never the right path ahead. Let me put it this way: I happen to think that my wife is one of the most amazing people on the planet. I think she's beautiful, smart, and supportive. I also think my children are incredible. They're kind, good people, who are growing into better people than I am. I also strongly believe I've got the best dog in the world. These aren't debates about work. We should all fully understand and appreciate that some points of view are more provocative than others, and we cannot discount the discomfort that can come from working with people who view the world differently than we do. That is one aspect of diverse and inclusive teams. It would be far easier if everyone thought like we do and valued what we value, but that wouldn't really be diversity. And focusing on how that diversity helps drive greater performance is how we turn something that might otherwise be considered a bug into a feature. When the goal is philosophical and ideological alignment, different perspectives can feel like a problem. When the goal is finding better answers to complex challenges, different experiences and perspectives is a solution. Effective culture just looks like high performance.

Let's consider two scenarios for how the ABCS model can be deployed, along with alternate scenarios showing what happens if even one element is missing. These two examples show up in the vast majority of organizations and have real implications for the health of the business. If one of these scenarios doesn't resonate with you, I'm pretty confident the other one will. And if you've had the fortune of not having experienced either of these situations just yet, hold on, because you probably aren't very far away from encountering one or both of these as you continue your leadership journey.

The first example shows how the ABCS model can be applied to weekly performance check-ins. The second example shows how the ABCS model can help an organization create a healthier pipeline of new ideas on a more frequent basis. By seeing the ABCS model used up close, I hope it's clear how it can help you transform your corner of the organization.

Company A Struggles with Weekly Check-Ins

In Company A, a particularly attentive senior leader begins to get signals that the performance cycle isn't producing the desired results. This manager is hearing from other leaders and individual contributors that the weekly check-in meetings, if they happen at all, are a waste of time. That alone is concerning. Feedback through engagement surveys is showing that employees are regularly leaving weekly check-in meetings with both a lack of clear guidance and direction, and with a sense that their managers are too busy to support their development goals and their performance goals. The company feels like it's regularly off-kilter, and the very process of setting goals has become a bit of a joke, because things are so poorly planned that most weeks feel as if they are filled with unplanned chaos more than they're filled with anything resembling a coherent plan.

This leader sees that they need to gather more information to better understand the root of the issue, and so they organize a small group of employees from various levels of the company. This group maps out the employee and leader journey as it relates to weekly check-ins, and how those are meant to feed up to an annual performance review. During this period of awareness building, the group discovers that one of the most frequently cited issues is a lack of dedicated time and consistency. Managers regularly schedule the meeting, then move it to accommodate other meetings; or employees come to the meeting prepared to discuss goals and objectives, and the meeting is overrun by daily priorities or more tactical business items. And so the preparation for the conversation is seen as a waste, and each time this happens it sends a signal to the employee that their check-in is not important.

The behavior that the team identifies is that the check-in meeting will be scheduled no less than two business days in advance, and that the time will only be moved or taken over in the most serious of situations, like sickness or business-critical priorities. This flexibility means that there is still some latitude for unavoidable circumstances, but the core behaviors of scheduling the meeting, planning for the meeting, and keeping the meeting are made clear and paramount.

The leader also knows that the clearer the meetings are, while not becoming rigid, the better. They make the effort to clarify key elements of the check-in meeting. They clarify what will happen during the check-in, describing in detail things that an observer could see, hear, record, or recount. For instance, they recognize that "paying attention" is not a behavior, and therefore seek out more specific behaviors. The leader gives crucial examples like making eye contact, shutting down their technology or setting their devices to "Do Not Disturb," and taking notes, and understands that these are the kinds of behaviors that signal that the leader is paying attention and minimizing distractions.

Now the leader spreads the word to other leaders, and begins building community. They share what they've found, why these behaviors are the ones they're going to try, and what the benefit will be to all parties. The leader invites perspective and questions, yet does not allow the detractors to hold up testing and getting feedback on what's working and what might still need to be tweaked.

After the behaviors have been articulated and shared with the broader work community, the leader now helps put fluid systems in place to support the desired changes. For instance, the leader enlists the help of the graphics department to make a simple sheet that leaders and their direct reports can fill out in advance of the check-in meeting. In addition, the entire division changes their calendars to reflect that check-in meetings are now considered protected time, not subject to the same changes and adjustments as other meetings. And perhaps as the groups gain more confidence and cycles, they will invest in a more fixed system, such as a technology platform that ties into the rest of their HR systems. Leaders may even be evaluated based on how regularly and thoroughly they complete their check-ins, with a recognition that greater engagement in check-ins leads to better performance and higher job satisfaction.

In this new state, check-ins are mutually beneficial experiences where employees get valuable time for development and feedback, and leaders gain a deeper understanding of their people and how things are going across the business. In these exchanges lies a real commitment to growth, communication, and collaboration. There's still work to do – this ABCS cycle won't solve everything – but it's having a positive impact, and that progress feels good and is translating to a stronger, healthier company.

That's the best-case scenario: everyone using the ABCS as it was intended. But now let's imagine a slightly different set of scenarios, as the company works through the process for the first time. While the changes may seem small, we can see how removing just one element at a time can quickly lead the entire effort to fall apart.

In a case where the scenario is devoid of Awareness, the leader forgoes gaining feedback and clarity about the actual problem. They are far less likely to discover that the root issue is commitment to the meetings, and perhaps instead follow their instincts and hypothesize that what's going wrong is a lack of clarity about the importance of check-ins. The leader engages in a communication campaign, with emails, content on the intranet, and well-laid presentations at company town halls. They try to get everyone on board, to build the community, but in fact what they do is continue to deepen the divide between employees and managers, because everyone agrees that the check-ins are important, but they're still not happening with planning, consistency, and without interruption. Building fluid or fixed systems that reinforce this debacle is just going to make it that much harder to unwind. This leader has thrown a dart at the board, and missed identifying the right behaviors.

In the case where the Behaviors element is missing, the leader delivers on the awareness and discovers the problem's root cause. But by jumping right to building community, the leader is galvanizing people around a problem, without offering the specific and concrete behaviors that will help address that problem. Now each manager is doing their own thing. They've been given the direction, "Be more present during check-ins," and confusion is rampant. Direct reports aren't sure what it means to be present, and so their expectations are all over the place. Leaders aren't sure what it means to be present, and so their behaviors are all over the place. An observer would have little to no idea what they're seeing, and the variance from check-in to check-in would be profound. This leader is likely to overcompensate by being too prescriptive about the systems, which is a classic mistake. When struggling leaders can't get the big things right, they lean heavily into the little things. Jumping straight to fixed systems and being anchored in the system elements that are not the most important behavior, this leader seems more like a micromanager than a leader. The mix of inconsistency where the behaviors matter, and inflexibility throughout the system, leads people to push back. The change doesn't hold, and things fall apart. Again.

When we play out this scenario missing Community, the leader gets the awareness right, and gets at the root of what matters. They also get the behaviors right, and can confidently and clearly explain the actions that will drive better outcomes. But they assume that being right is enough to bring people along. They avoid doing the hard work of sharing, informing, and creating partnerships. This leader assumes that everyone will see the brilliance of the solution and be eager to get on board. But that's not how people work. And so when this leader tries to embed the behaviors and launch the systems, they are constantly hampered by questions, concerns, and stepping back to try to explain to groups they missed and partners they ignored, all while dealing with both passive and active resistance.

Lastly, if they ignore the Systems in this version of events, we see the leaders get it all right, just up to the point where it comes to putting in place the surrounding mechanisms that will make the behaviors more likely to stick. Without the tools, scheduling guidance, rewards, and penalties, the check-ins work for a while, but then life gets in the way. Without the change efforts tied into the rest of the organization, they feel separate and distinct, and therefore disposable. When things are calm, easy, and ideal, leaders demonstrate the desired behaviors. But when things are busy, tough, and suboptimal, leaders discard the behaviors, because it's easier not to do these things.

Company B Faces a Crisis of Innovation

In Company B, we find a leader who manages a call center. This manager is busy, taxed, and struggling to keep customers happy, supervisors at bay, and call center employees from falling behind schedule. While this call center manager would like to think that they're at least an above-average leader, they recognize that their workload, priorities, and the non-stop demands of reacting to customer needs are making it difficult to show up for their people in some of the ways they would like. One of the most prevalent ways this leader would like to support their team – and a bit selfishly support themself – is through getting more ideas from their people about ways they can better innovate to handle more calls, reduce customer complaints, and streamline processes. This leader has read a number of great articles about inviting creativity and the benefits that can bring for engagement and productivity, but they're at a bit of a loss for where to begin.

Adding to the ever-growing list of challenges, turnover at the call center is quite high, which means that by the time they've made a connection with an employee, that employee may be on their way to another department or out the door to another company. So this manager is stuck in a cycle of bringing people on, getting them trained just enough to do their jobs, and then wishing them well on their future endeavors. A few employees have stuck around for longer than normal, and of that group there are a few who are passionate and motivated, a few who are probably staying because it's easier than finding another job, and a few who are just barely getting by. This leader knows there are a host of things they could go after, but they want to start with soliciting more ideas because they know that even within this environment, which measures productivity by the minute, there are things they could be doing better. But this leader feels like they're too close to the problems, and too embedded in the management of it all, to see everything with an honest lens.

This leader starts with Awareness. They sit down with some of their employees and ask them why they think others aren't sharing their ideas. Then the leader asks employees why they're not sharing their own ideas. Each conversation provides another piece of information about the obstacles, the challenges, and the perceptions regarding whether leadership truly wants opinions, or if they're just pretending to care. These handful of conversations are insightful, validating some things the leader already perceived, and turning some other things around completely. This leader reads articles about how different high paced environments with some similarity have handled this kind of communication challenge. They read about automobile assembly lines across different countries and cultures. They read a bit about emergency rooms, airplane cockpits, and battlefield communications. While each of these conditions are distinct and different from the problem they face, they find some similarity in how innovation and idea generation happens during the rare downtimes, in order to prepare and optimize for the peak times.

When it comes to Behaviors, this leader is clear and unambiguous. Among a variety of behaviors that could work, they suggest to their team that they begin with the behavior: "Every month, during a 25-minute meeting, you'll bring three ideas to our conversation: one thing you can do differently, one thing I can do differently, and one thing the company can do differently, to make this a more effective and efficient workplace." The leader tests this against questions of whether someone could see or hear this happening, and decides that for a start, this is the right behavior to test.

When it comes to building Community, the leader takes a commune approach, and recognizes that they don't need very many other parties to support this work. The leader and their team can deploy this on their own, test it on their own, and evolve it mostly on their own. As such, they're deliberate about not going too broad too soon, and instead build the community on their own team first, with a plan for how to share it more fully if and when the time presents itself, like when they hear their boss or their peers lamenting their own lack of feedback or suggestions from their teams.

Lastly, there are the Systems. The leader knows that some of the key fluid systems revolve around scheduling the meetings and ensuring each person has adequate time away from the phone. They consider introducing an email template to capture the three questions they and the team have identified. In doing so, they recognize that the form is a supporting mechanism, while asking and answering the three questions is the root of the solution to the problem. They don't confuse the system for the behavior. Looking ahead, this leader can even see a future where perhaps the monthly suggestions from across the call center are run through an analysis to find top themes and trends, but they know that's a bit of a ways off. For now they're eager to get this new behavior embedded in the team, and see what works and what may need to be adjusted.

Just like with our leader from Company A, this ABCS cycle doesn't solve everything; nor was it meant to. Primarily, it gives employees a greater sense of autonomy and contribution to the workplace. What the leader gets is a window into what people are thinking, and how they believe the call center can deliver better results for all stakeholders, including employees. And this leader has a chance to bring ideas to the surface, and at the same time they can explain why some ideas are more feasible than others, which creates dynamic and interesting conversations between the leader and the team. By asking about the individual and the company, the leader creates shared accountability, instead of just inviting finger-pointing or venting. They identified an opportunity, a solution, a way to bring others along, and a system to reduce friction.

The reason for this leader's success with implementing their new behaviors rests squarely on their strong execution of the ABCS model. If they had rushed through or skipped a step, the outcome would most certainly be different. Like the previous example, let's see how missing just one step in the process makes it harder to find success overall.

If this leader were to skip the Awareness step, they would jump straight to dictating the behaviors that the call center employees should start to adopt. The odds that the leader would stumble onto the right behaviors are quite low. Without the time spent talking with the team, researching what's actually going on, why it's happening, and what others have done to address similar challenges, this leader is bound to select behaviors based on unnecessarily incomplete information. They will struggle to explain to others why these behaviors are rooted in an understanding of what is happening, and not simply another example of a leader impressing their opinions onto others. They are bound to experience resistance along the remaining steps of the ABCS model, and their ability to build a strong community and select the right supporting systems is going to be compromised.

This leader is running headlong into a frustrating experience. As my father has often said, borrowing from others, "If you don't know where you're going, any road will take you there." This leader, by skipping Awareness, has less of an idea of where they are going. This all might take the form of this leader doing some general observation about why others in the call center aren't speaking up, determining without consultation or exploration that everyone just needs to volunteer more ideas, and then doing their best to sell that to others. A failure to understand what's getting in the way inevitably leads to a failure to address what's getting in the way.

Should this leader forgo Behaviors, their path to ineffectiveness is different, but no less tragic. In this version of events, the leader does the work to identify during the Awareness stage what is missing and why. They do their research and pull great ideas from around them. Where the leader will stumble is that without clear behaviors, the call center employees start to contribute their ideas in a wide variety of ways. Some drop in on the leader unannounced with a grand new idea. Others pause taking customer calls to jot down an insight they've had. Others send off a half dozen emails a week, all with suggestions for what everyone else should be doing differently. These employees are becoming frustrated at the lack of response and lack of activity to address their concerns, so they conclude that the leader doesn't actually care, and was only asking to look like they were invested in employees. The initiative falls apart almost as quickly as it was put together, all because of the uncertainty around what was actually being asked of people.

"Contribute more ideas" made sense in theory, but in practice, without specificity, each person's unique point of view led to unique and disparate actions.

Without Community, this leader is on a proverbial island. Despite recognizing that this situation was more of a commune than a neighborhood, when this leader failed to bring together those who were not part of the initial information gathering, they also failed to galvanize the team around the vision of what was to come. By either ignoring the action of building a community, or by attempting to build the community in ways that ignored the Key 3, like having confusing language or incomprehensible marketing, they failed to build the coalition that could keep this work going.

While a small cohort of call center employees rallied around the behaviors, it wasn't enough to change the dynamics or the culture. Trying to embed the behaviors in new systems, whether fluid or fixed, only leads to people exercising their creativity by figuring out how to work around the systems. Energy that could be spent generating and sharing new ideas is rather spent generating and sharing new workarounds. The leader either winds up defeated and forfeits the initiative, or digs in their heels and makes the mandates even more rigid. Either path leads to frustration and moves the leader further from the initial goal of engaging more employees, more often.

In the absence of Systems, it's all going well for the call center leader and their employees, until another priority emerges. Without systems to fall back on when times are busy or challenging, the new behavior never quite takes hold.

The leader can launch and relaunch the initiative many times over, but it always stops in the face of new responsibilities or when times get even remotely busy. This leader and their team feel the highs of what it can feel like when things are going well and everyone is sharing their ideas, but they are also keenly aware that this sits squarely on the periphery of what the company cares about, because as soon as something else emerges, soliciting ideas goes away. It may not be all for naught, because some of the ideas that are generated may be supported and adopted, but knowing that hearing from employees really only matters until there are other things to do sends a definitive message, which the call center employees hear loud and clear.

These are just two examples. They barely scratch the surface of all the ways the ABCS model can help you create a stronger, healthier, more resilient culture. Use these examples as a starting point for thinking about the challenges your team or department faces. Identify what doesn't seem to be working that you'd like to build more awareness about. Focus on how you could start educating yourself on the problem. Get clear on whom you could talk to that would help create greater clarity around the challenges you are facing, but not yet addressing. Doing this ongoing introspection, with genuine curiosity, is an important first step toward making any worthwhile change.

A natural question to ask is why all of this is worth the time and effort. You're likely surrounded by leaders who have done just fine without putting in the additional rigor to understand the problem, clarify the behaviors, build the community, and embed the actions in the systems. They may have been promoted, rewarded, and probably sleep soundly, and aren't doing the work you've signed up to do. So you may inquire why you should bother to go above and beyond. A reasonable leader can wonder what the payoff is for embracing the ABCS model.

There is a tremendous difference between being a manager and being a leader, and an equally big divide between being a leader and being an effective leader. Most managers are primarily concerned with achieving the goals that are set in front of them. They've been told to achieve something, and their energy is spent on achieving that objective. Many leaders are concerned with inspiring and developing individuals to achieve goals and growth.

They see people as an investment, and believe that by supporting and empowering them, their people will achieve the current goals, as well as be prepared for the goals that will come up in the future.

An effective leader is concerned with building a culture of high performance. They see that development and investment without output and performance is incomplete. They know that a diverse and inclusive team that isn't also performing is a waste of talent. If your goal is to have a positive impact on your business and your team, to deliver greater outputs for your business and your team, and to find a deep sense of fulfillment doing the hard work of building your business and your team, then this is the right path to walk.

On an organizational level, companies that embed the ABCS into their ways of working benefit in two major ways compared to companies that forgo the model: clarity and boundaries. Both clarity and boundaries fundamentally change the way a company feels and functions.

Clarity comes in the organization's ability to clearly and confidently describe the problems, along with a plan for how they are addressing them. Even at the stage when the company is still investigating the problems, a company that has embraced the ABCS will have the credibility to let employees know that it's using its well-researched findings to make important changes to how things are done.

Most companies can't, and don't, make these kinds of commitments to their employees because they don't know what's going wrong, and they're not taking the right steps to find out.

If you've worked for any length of time, you've probably felt these effects. It can feel like confusion and disillusionment over what the company considers important, because things are raised and not resolved, or started and not sustained. It can feel like frustration over things not getting done at all, or the stress of bureaucracy making it so that progress is best measured over years. And over time it may feel like cynicism and disengagement, because what becomes pervasive is a feeling that nothing will ever get done, and you might as well make the best of things in your own tiny orbit, while avoiding everything and everyone on the outside.

But imagine the relief of working at a company where you can confidently show up to work each day and know that the right problems are being addressed, taken seriously, and communicated clearly. Let's understand this doesn't mean that work becomes perfect, where every action is met with praise and celebration. There are still stressors – there will always be stressors – but they are confined to the work itself. In working for such a company, you aren't forced to deal with the stress of dysfunction, personal disagreements, or ideological issues that are beyond the job you were selected to do.

This is where boundaries, the second benefit, come in. You get the opportunity to show up as yourself, with all your unique and valuable experiences and ways of thinking, and everyone recognizes the difference between your whole self and your whole *work self*. The organization recognizes what work is really for, so you and everyone else are only asked to leverage the parts of you that help you perform in your role. You and your colleagues understand what issues aren't helpful or appropriate because you're clear what you're there to do.

This shared understanding allows people to focus on their job. It doesn't preclude friendships or getting to know each other. It doesn't mean that we have to show up to work as automatons or be emotionless, yet it doesn't presume the opposite end of that spectrum either. These boundaries empower you and those around you to raise pointed concerns if you feel an aspect of your identity isn't being leveraged in the right way, based on the scope of your role and the outputs you're looking to achieve. This is what it looks like to create a culture where people can do their best work without feeling like they have to defend basic aspects of their humanity, or check out entirely and suppress who they are. Instead, we can show up to work knowing what's expected of us, our team, and how each person offers their own unique contributions to the overall success of the group. If you're responsible for leading others, guiding their growth and development, while also moving the organization forward, you can be part of the change.

Companies are communities of human beings working together to provide value. That's what they always have been. Yet over the years, the perceived role of a company has swung between taking advantage of employees by expecting them to give their all and receive relatively little in return, and employees expecting the company to be the driver of societal progress, while the employees become less loyal to the mission of the company.

Ultimately, when we strip it all down, the vast majority of work is done by humans, working with, and for, other humans. Your ability to create the conditions in which those humans can perform at their peak is the most basic responsibility of leadership. But let's go beyond the basics and aspire for more. Let's help everyone do their best work.

Epilogue

Building cultures that win.

One of the first times I put the ABCS model into practice, I didn't even know it was happening, or that there was the flicker of a model being born.

At the time, I was just kind of stumbling along, making decisions, and reacting to what was happening around me. And while that level of luck and serendipity happens from time to time, what I benefit from now, and what I am excited about for you, is the ability to look ahead, plan for the desired outcome, and intentionally bring along a team of skilled partners to deliver strong results.

It was 2010. I was working on a large training team, and my company was feverishly opening new retail stores as part of a global expansion. In some instances, we were expanding into countries where we didn't yet have a presence. Instead of expanding our training delivery team, a collection of our leaders came up with the unconventional idea to have trainers come from existing retail stores and help with training the new store teams. These "guest trainers" weren't professional trainers, but they were people with the appetite and aptitude to learn. They were successful employees who knew the company culture, understood how the stores operated, and spoke the languages of the countries where we were expanding.

The idea to bring on these temporary trainers was well received, and I, alongside some of the best people with whom I've ever had the fortune to work, were responsible for building key elements of the program, such as making sure that the temporary trainers were prepared to go out into the world and successfully open new stores. Before they could do that, though, we needed to select them, and train them on how to train others. Facilitation, presentation, planning, logistics, and a host of other skills were needed, and we had a limited time to bring this group of dozens of trainers from around the world to our headquarters and give them the resources they needed to deliver great experiences through these store openings.

One of the first things we realized after bringing the guest trainers together was that many of them had never traveled outside of their home country before, and all of them wanted to do a great job. But for many of the trainers this excitement quickly turned to anxiety. They began putting enormous amounts of pressure on themselves, and it started to show in their demeanor and their performance. Our permanent team of instructors would give the trainers content to prepare – similar to an actor practicing their lines for a role – and each trainer's task was to study the content and come to a session ready to deliver the training. This is where pressure turned to stress. Several of these trainers, who were so confident and competent in other aspects of their jobs, struggled to deliver the content. And so we paused and sought to understand what exactly was happening.

This was our Awareness step.

Instead of assuming that we'd selected incorrectly, or that the trainers were incapable of completing this assignment, we asked, "Why?" Why were they struggling? Why was this stressful? We listened, and we learned that it was the feedback process. After each person delivered their content, the instructors provided feedback. And the feedback started with observations from our instructors saying what went well and what they'd suggest the trainer do differently. While the feedback was always meant to be supportive, and was delivered with care and positive intent, we discovered that having the instructors go first gave the instructors ownership over the feedback. Essentially, this meant we were robbing the trainers of the opportunity to call out what they already knew they would do differently. They were hearing feedback about things they had already identified during their practice session.

We knew we had to do something, but what?

Building culture is unpredictable and never ending. It's unpredictable because culture is about people, and people reject being constrained or neatly defined. People, teams, and culture will continue to flow and change, and any good set of principles and practices will include enough flexibility to account for that flow and change. And it's never ending because building a culture is not a finite activity. There is no finish line, no stopping point, no moment where you can proclaim success and put it all to rest. Culture is not a finite game with fixed rules and a score to be kept. This means that building a culture of high performance along with the building blocks of DEI is not a sprint or even a marathon; it's the very exercise itself. As long as the company exists, you will be refining the culture.

You can think of what you gain by using the ABCS as the fuel to keep you going, as you explore new and better ways to set up the culture to support your goals. There will be obstacles and frustrations; those are to be expected. There will be successes and celebrations; those are to be embraced. More than anything, you need to give yourself and those around you the grace to let this work take the time that it requires. At first you may slowly begin to see things being done differently, before you begin to pick up momentum. That momentum will take a somewhat unique form, because you'll also begin to notice that the actions you take are empowering other people in the organization.

What this means is that you'll address actions more than you'll address demographics, and this is a key point because many modern DEI programs do the opposite, at times to poor results.

Instead of fixing issues for a particular group, you'll fix issues for the entire organization. Rather than trying to lift up one group at a time, your ability to get to the root of problems will allow you to lift lots of people at once. Or, to quote a favored saying from another one of my past mentors, "A rising tide lifts all boats." You'll start to see that visible or salient problems in one group in the organization are usually invisible or emerging problems with other groups, and that with a little bit of digging to understand the true scale of the issue, you can deliver a positive experience to more people all at once.

This is the true promise of culture done well, and the true value of the ABCS model.

While you are lifting up whole teams and departments, you'll notice another benefit of building these skills and seeing them succeed over time is that you and those around you are willing and able to make faster decisions. Knowing that you've described and researched the issue, identified clear behaviors, built the community, and crafted the supporting systems will give you the confidence to act decisively.

Much of what passes for organizational dysfunction can be traced to indecision: a team's or leader's unwillingness to take action and boldly move toward an outcome. As you get comfortable with the ABCS model, and adept at moving through the cycles with even greater pace and dexterity, you'll notice an increased willingness to push through ambiguity and make a commitment. Your intuition – that is, a deep understanding of your organization, honed through multiple cycles of the process – will begin to take over.

So, what commitment did my colleagues and I make to help the guest trainers receive better feedback?

After we identified the problem in our Awareness phase, we moved confidently into the Behaviors phase. We knew we needed to do something differently, and we had a hypothesis to test. *Could the problem lie with the order in which feedback is given?* We thought it might. So, we came up with a new behavior. When a trainer finished their practice, the first thing we'd ask is, "What feedback do you have for yourself?" That way, instead of hearing from the instructors first, trainers initiated the feedback process.

Most times, they immediately went into what went wrong and what they would adjust or do differently in the future. They owned their feedback, and thereby owned the feedback process. And the response was immediately more positive. Trainers felt empowered, observers gave more specific and useful advice, performance increased, and confidence climbed.

Now we were in the Community stage.

We made sure everyone who would interact with the trainers during their practice sessions knew about this new procedure – that trainers always went first with their feedback for themselves – and we shared why. The community saw the benefit, and was happy to support this new behavior. But then we realized something else, and needed to adjust the behavior.

You may have noticed that I said the trainers "immediately went into what went wrong and what they would adjust."

What went wrong.

They were so focused on highlighting the elements they'd flubbed or the question they wished they'd asked differently during their practice. But starting with the negative felt wrong. Our behavior was more right than before, but it could be tweaked again to be even more effective. And so we edited the behavior. Now, after a trainer finished their practice, they would give themselves feedback, and they had to start with what they did well. If a trainer accidentally started listing what they didn't like about their delivery, we'd gently yet firmly stop them, and redirect them to start with the good stuff. If they joked that everything fell apart and they didn't do anything well, we'd push them to find the behaviors that they'd want to repeat, because there always were things to highlight.

Now we had a behavior that was proving even more effective for teaching and supporting our trainers, and preparing them to deliver on their objectives.

Then came the Systems phase.

For starters, we changed our feedback forms. Instead of putting the challenges at the top of the form, we started with what went well. Even that seemingly small change reinforced that we should lead with support and positivity, yet did not shy away from giving full and robust feedback and advice. We also changed our debriefs at the end of the day to follow a similar format. Trainer self-feedback, and starting with the positive, became the way all of our processes flowed. And then it made its way to the permanent members of the training team, and then to how we trained and supported employees in a variety of training contexts. The first temporary trainer team was wildly successful by every metric.

Through stumbling onto the ABCS method in this instance, we changed how people experienced a whole program, and what they took away from that experience. We repeated the temporary trainer program many times over the years, and as we continued to evolve it, I would often welcome new trainers by telling them, "You're not here to prove yourself, you're here to improve yourself," and we could literally see people's shoulders relax just a bit, as they eased into a high-performance team.

This ABCS cycle didn't just solve a problem for how to enter new markets in 2010. It helped spawn a brand-new culture of support and learning, totally transforming how significant portions of the company operated. By conventional DEI metrics, you might say we made the feedback process more inclusive, heightened the trainers' sense of belonging, and increased their sense of equity in the process by allowing them to own their feedback. And that is all true. But turning each of those individual dials wasn't the sole purpose of the work. The purpose was to strengthen the business's operations and support a new strategy. And yet, even with a performance-focused mission, people came away feeling more confident, respected, and valued as employees than when they walked in. The culture improved, and so did the business. This is the true promise of the ABCS.

I hope I haven't given you the impression along the course of this book that I have these elements completely nailed, and have reached a point where the ABCS model just flows naturally and effortlessly. It's more fluid than it was years ago, yet it still requires intention and effort. I presume that will always be the case. As you know, culture building isn't easy. But it is important, because work is important. And the ABCS model is something that I've refined for myself over two decades of working to build and be part of world-class cultures that accomplish amazing things.

Many leaders will say that they care about the culture of their organization. Fewer leaders are willing to do the hard work with others to build and maintain cultures of excellence and performance. And even fewer leaders are willing to invest in themselves and their leadership capabilities to increase their team's likelihood of success. Congratulations on taking yet another step on the journey toward building and maintaining an amazing organization that infuses culture as a means to high performance and excellence.

I'll continue to be on that same journey of culture and evolution with you, and I'm excited to have another ABCS practitioner out there, helping everyone they meet to lead teams that win.

Notes

Introduction

1. a. David Rock and Heidi Grant, "Why Diverse Teams Are Smarter," *Harvard Business Review*, November 4, 2016, https://hbr.org/2016/11/why-diverse-teams-are-smarter.

b. Adam D. Galinsky et al., "Maximizing the Gains and Minimizing the Pains of Diversity," *Perspectives on Psychological Science* 10, no. 6 (November 1, 2015): 742–48, https://doi.org/10.1177/1745691615598513.

c. Naomi Ellemers and Floortje Rink, "Diversity in Work Groups," *Current Opinion in Psychology* 11 (October 1, 2016): 49–53, https://doi.org/10.1016/j.copsyc.2016.06.001.

Chapter 1. A Big Misunderstanding

1. a. Steven Pinker, *Enlightenment Now: The Case for Reason, Science, Humanism, and Progress* (Penguin, 2018).

b. Max Roser, "Proof That Life Is Getting Better for Humanity, in 5 Charts," *Vox*, December 23, 2016, https://www.vox.com/the-big-idea/2016/12/23/14062168/history-global-conditions-charts-life-span-poverty.

c. Robert Muggah, "The Maps That Show Life Is Slowly Getting Better," *The Guardian*, October 19, 2020, https://www.theguardian.com/world/2020/oct/17/the-maps-that-show-life-is-slowly-getting-better.

2. a. David Milliken, "Gloomy youth pull US and western Europe down global happiness ranking," *Reuters*, March 21, 2024, https://www.reuters.com/lifestyle/gloomy-youth-pull-us-western-europe-down-global-happiness-ranking-2024-03-20/.

   b. Office of the Assistant Secretary for Health (OASH), "New Surgeon General Advisory Raises Alarm About the Devastating Impact of the Epidemic of Loneliness and Isolation in the United States," *HHS.Gov*, May 3, 2023, https://www.hhs.gov/about/news/2023/05/03/new-surgeon-general-advisory-raises-alarm-about-devastating-impact-epidemic-loneliness-isolation-united-states.html.

   c. Rob Wijnberg, "The Great Paradox of Our Time: Everything Is Both Better and Worse Than Ever Before," *The Correspondent*, November 7, 2019, https://thecorrespondent.com/104/the-great-paradox-of-our-time-everything-is-both-better-and-worse-than-ever-before.

3. a. "Lloyd Trotter, a GE Executive Using Best Practices for Productivity Improvements." *VINE. Very Informal Newsletter on Library Automation/VINE* 38, no. 3 (August 29, 2008). https://doi.org/10.1108/vine.2008.28738caf.001.

Chapter 2. The ABCS of Culture

1. a. "APA Dictionary of Psychology," n.d., https://dictionary.apa.org/naive-realism.

   b. "Cognitive Biases Can Affect Experts' Judgments: A Broad Descriptive Model and Systematic Review in One Domain," *American Psychological Association*, n.d. https://www.apa.org/pubs/highlights/spotlight /issue-235.

c. Ben Yagoda, "Cognitive Biases and the Human Brain," *The Atlantic*, August 7, 2018, https://www .theatlantic.com/magazine/archive/2018/09/cognitive-bias/565775/.

2. a. "Teamwork Vs. Individual Work: Which Is Better? – Knowledge at Wharton," *Knowledge at Wharton*, April 26, 2024, https://knowledge.wharton.upenn .edu/podcast/knowledge-at-wharton-podcast/are-teams-better-than-individuals-at-getting-work-done/.

b. Gareth Cook, "Why We Are Wired to Connect," *Scientific American*, February 20, 2024, https:// www.scientificamerican.com/article/why-we-are-wired-to-connect/.

Chapter 3. Start with Awareness

1. a. Mark D. Faries, "Why We Don't 'Just Do It,'" *American Journal of Lifestyle Medicine* 10, no. 5 (June 22, 2016): 322–29, https://doi.org/10.1177/15598276 16638017.

b. Subhash C. Kundu, Sandeep Kumar, and Kusum Lata, "Effects of Perceived Role Clarity on Innovative Work Behavior: A Multiple Mediation Model," *RAUSP Management Journal* 55, no. 4 (November 1, 2019): 457–72, https://doi.org/10.1108/rausp-04-2019-0056.

Chapter 5. Behaviors Over Beliefs

1. a. Barry Schwartz, *The Paradox of Choice: Why More Is Less* (Harper Collins, 2003).

Chapter 6. Behaviors Practice

1. a. Steven Pinker, *The Sense of Style: The Thinking Person's Guide to Writing in the 21st Century* (Penguin, 2014).

2. a. John Steele, "'We Are Visual Animals, Driven by Images' - Nautilus," *Nautilus*, September 12, 2022, https://nautil.us/we-are-visual-animals-driven-by-images-234909/.

   b. Joel Pearson, "The Human Imagination: The Cognitive Neuroscience of Visual Mental Imagery," *Nature Reviews. Neuroscience* 20, no. 10 (August 5, 2019): 624–34, https://doi.org/10.1038/s41583-019-0202-9.

3. a. Adam L. Alter and Daniel M. Oppenheimer, "Predicting Short-term Stock Fluctuations by Using Processing Fluency," *Proceedings of the National Academy of Sciences of the United States of America* 103, no. 24 (June 13, 2006): 9369–72, https://doi.org/10.1073/pnas.0601071103.

   b. NeuroLeadership Institute, "The Power of Fluency With Dr. Adam Alter," February 7, 2020, https://www.youtube.com/watch?v=hUBK9tOJCKE.

Chapter 8. Community Practice

1. a. Van Boven Leaf, George Loewenstein, and David Dunning, "The Illusion of Courage in Social Predictions: Underestimating the Impact of Fear of Embarrassment on Other People," 2005, https://papers.ssrn.com/sol3/papers.cfm?abstract_id=1532569.

   b. Steven Samuel, Geoff G Cole, and Madeline J Eacott, "Two Independent Sources of Difficulty in Perspective-taking/Theory of Mind Tasks," *Psychonomic Bulletin*

& *Review* 27, no. 6 (August 10, 2020): 1341–47, https://doi.org/10.3758/s13423-020-01789-6.

2. a. James K. Sebenius, "Six Habits of Merely Effective Negotiators," *Harvard Business Review*, April 2001, https://hbr.org/2001/04/six-habits-of-merely-effective-negotiators.

   b. David A. Lax and James K. Sebenius, "Interests: The Measure of Negotiation," *Negotiation Journal* 2, no. 1 (January 1, 1986): 73–92, https://doi.org/10.1007/bf00998936.

3. a. Jim Collins, *Good to Great: Why Some Companies Make the Leap . . . and Others Don't* (Harper Collins, 2001).

Chapter 9. Systems Cement the Change

1. a. Roy Baumeister et al., "Is Willpower a Limited Resource?," *American Psychological Association*, n.d., https://www.apa.org/topicswillpower-limited.pdf.

   b. Brian Resnick, "Self Control Is Overrated. Willpower Is Too.," *Vox*, January 2, 2020, https://www.vox.com/science-and-health/2018/1/15/16863374/willpower-overrated-self-control-psychology.

   c. Daniel R. Schweitzer et al., "Self-control, Limited Willpower and Decision Fatigue in Healthcare Settings," *Internal Medicine Journal* 53, no. 6 (June 1, 2023): 1076–80, https://doi.org/10.1111/imj.16121.

2. a. American Medical Association, "What Doctors Wish Patients Knew About Decision Fatigue," *American Medical Association*, November 19, 2021, https://www.ama-assn.org/delivering-care/public-health/what-doctors-wish-patients-knew-about-decision-fatigue.

b. Kathleen Elkins, "Richard Branson Wears 'the Same Pair of Jeans Every Day'—here's How It Could Contribute to His Success," CNBC, June 7, 2019, https://www.cnbc.com/2019/06/07/why-successful-people-wear-the-same-thing-every-day.html.

c. James Clear, "How Willpower Works: Decision Fatigue and How to Avoid Bad Choices," James Clear, July 20, 2018, https://jamesclear.com/willpower-decision-fatigue.

Chapter 10. Systems Practice

1. a. Michael G Vann, "Of Rats, Rice, and Race: The Great Hanoi Rat Massacre, an Episode in French Colonial History," *French Colonial History* 4, no. 1 (January 1, 2003): 191–203, https://doi.org/10.1353/fch.2003.0027.

2. a. Conor Kenny, "'The Single Biggest Problem in Communication Is the Illusion That It Has Taken Place,'" *The Irish Times*, November 9, 2020, https://www.irishtimes.com/culture/books/the-single-biggest-problem-in-communication-is-the-illusion-that-it-has-taken-place-1.4404586#.

3. a. "How Plan Design Tweaks Can Boost Participant Saving Rates," *Vanguard*, n.d., https://corporate.vanguard.com/content/corporatesite/us/en/corp/articles/how-plan-design-tweaks-boost-participant-saving-rates.html.

b. "What Will Get People to Save More for Retirement? Letting Them 'opt Out,'" *Fortune*, February 19, 2020, https://fortune.com/2020/02/20/opt-out-fixing-retirement-savings/.

Acknowledgments

First my thanks need to go to my amazing family. You have always been equal parts supportive and uplifting, and appropriately humbling. Whenever I thought I wasn't enough of an expert to write this book, you gave me the nurturing and supportive reminders that I needed to persevere, and whenever I came close to getting too full of myself, you hastily brought any shadow of an ego back down to earth. Dad, Mom, Sandra, Kevyn, and Connor, your faith and confidence is a gift, and I appreciate it with all of my heart. Grandma, Jamal, and Mike, you've always been there, and I know you always will be.

To Chris Weller, without whom this book most certainly would not have happened. Chris, you helped me navigate the process, get thoughts out of my head, pushed back on ideas that didn't make sense yet, and helped draw out important concepts. Not only would this book not be anywhere near as good, but without your support, partnership, expertise, and collaboration, this book would not even be complete. All of the best parts have your imprint on them, and all the least awesome parts are probably things you tried to talk me out of anyway.

Zach Schisgal and the team at Wiley. You believed and invested.

Janet Stovall, Jay Van Bavel, Mary Slaughter, and James Logan. Thank you for reading the early drafts and making this better, smarter, and tighter. If everyone had feedback and friendship like you offer, the world would be a better place.

My team at Akamai. Angie, Belle, Hema, Julia, Kara, Magda, Sharnali, and Steven, I am fortunate to work with a team of individuals who exemplify every good concept in this book, and a team that pushes me to be a better leader. This book is a how-to guide for helping others get closer to achieving what you all do.

To the amazing leaders from whom I've learned so much over the years. Anthony Williams, Denise Young-Smith, Ginger Mollo, Matt Marcotte, Rebecca Zehrung, and Wendy Beckman. Each of you was the leader I needed at the moment that I had the fortune of working with you, and I carry your contributions into every interaction, and every page of this book.

Anne-Marie Summers, who saw enough in me to say yes to my MBA application at UNC. You changed the course of my education, my career, and my life. I'll always have a place for UNC because of you.

And of course, my amazing dog, Chewie. You know exactly when I need you to curl up next to me while I'm writing. You know when I need a break, and pull me away for a walk outside. When you decide to write a book, I'll return the favors. Until then we'll have to settle for stomach rubs and too many treats.

About the Author

Khalil Smith is the vice president of Inclusion, Diversity, and Engagement at Akamai Technologies, a cloud computing company that powers and protects life online. In his role Khalil and his team are responsible for a host of employee-focused work, including employer branding, employee resource groups, employee listening, and corporate philanthropy. Before joining Akamai, Khalil led Consulting, Practices, and Research at the NeuroLeadership Institute, a consulting firm that leverages research and science to support companies around the world with their culture change efforts. Khalil also spent more than 14 years at Apple Inc., much of that time focused on training and development across Apple retail.

Khalil has written and spoken extensively about corporate culture and employee engagement, talking with companies, colleges, and universities across the world, and with leadership teams across a wide variety of size, industry, and maturity. His writing has been featured in publications such as *Harvard Business Review*, *Forbes*, *strategy + business*, and *Business Insider*.

Khalil received a Master of Business Administration (MBA) from the University of North Carolina, with a focus on Leadership and Strategy. Khalil also received a Master of Science in Negotiation and Conflict Resolution from Columbia University.

Khalil married his high school sweetheart, Sandra. Together they've had the fortune to raise two wonderful sons, Kevyn and Connor, and one wonderful dog Chewie (short for Chewbacca). They live in Chapel Hill, North Carolina.

Chris Weller is the founder of 1-Across, a ghostwriting and editing services firm that works with Fortune 500 executives, *New York Times* best-selling social scientists, visionary entrepreneurs, and other thought leaders to change how people see the world. A former reporter and editor, Chris's writing has appeared in *The Atlantic*, *Harvard Business Review*, *Newsweek*, *Fast Company*, *Business Insider*, and more. He is also the co-creator of the 2020 documentary *Spelling the Dream* on Netflix.

Index